50 Activities for Teaching Emotional Intelligence
The Best From Innerchoice Publishing

Level II: Middle School

Introduction and Theory
by
Dianne Schilling

Innerchoice Publishing, Torrance, California 90505

Cover Design: Doug Armstrong Graphic Design

Illustrations: Roger Johnson, Zoe Wentz, and Dianne Schilling

INNERCHOICE PUBLISHING
P.O. BOX 1185
TORRANCE, CALIFORNIA 90505
Tel. (310) 816-3085 Fax (310) 816-3092

Contents

Over the last decade or so "wars" have been proclaimed, in turn, on teen pregnancy dropping out, drugs, and most recently violence. The trouble with such campaigns, though, is that they come too late, after the targeted problem has reached epidemic proportions and taken firm root in the lives of the young. They are crisis intervention, the equivalent of solving a problem by sending an ambulance to the rescue rather than giving an inoculation that would ward off the disease in the first place. Instead of more such "wars," what we need is to follow the logic of prevention, offering our children the skills for facing life that will increase their chances of avoiding any and all of these fates.

—Daniel Goleman

How to Use . . .
50 Activities for Teaching Emotional Intelligence

Inspiration and Origins

This activity guide is a collection of the most popular and effective emotional literacy activities offered by Innerchoice Publishing over the past ten years. The activities have been compiled expressly for the purpose of helping you apply the theory and recommendations of authorities in the field of brain-based education and emotional learning, including behavioral scientist and best-selling author Daniel Goleman (*Emotional Intelligence: Why It Can Matter More Than IQ*).

Like many educators, Goleman views "the curriculum" as a plan for ongoing comprehensive age-appropriate lessons taught school wide. Based on this definition, he is correct in concluding that very few schools currently have an emotional intelligence curriculum. Goleman asserts, "In theory, there is no reason why such a curriculum could not be taught in every school nationwide. It already exists in many, but only in bits and pieces...not as a fully developed, step-by-step curriculum."

Over the years, Innerchoice Publishing has contributed hundreds of "bits," "pieces" and fully-developed programs to thousands of schools throughout the country. You are invited to use this newest contribution to the EQ curricular mosaic as:

- the core of your emotional literacy curriculum

- a specialized EQ supplement to your existing curriculum

The bottom line is, don't neglect or take for granted the emotional life of your students. Feelings, self-awareness, life skills, conflict management, self-esteem, and all of the other developmental areas now identified as affecting emotional intelligence are critically important. An impressive array of brain-based research supports the validity of time and energy spent by educators in these domains. Emotions are not unruly remnants of stone-age survival to be hushed and otherwise ignored while we develop cognitive skills. Emotions drive our behavior, shape our values, and predispose us to choose one course of action over others. Emotional and rational skills are equally important interdependent components of human intelligence.

Unit Organization

The ten units in this guide each contain five activities, and comprise a complete emotional literacy curriculum. They are:

• *Self-awareness*

Knowing the likes, dislikes, hopes, preferences, cultural heritage, talents, shortcomings, and other uniquenesses that make up the individual. Becoming aware of inner and outer states and processes.

• *Managing Feelings*

Building a vocabulary for feelings; knowing the relationship between thoughts, feelings and actions; accurately reading feeling cues in others and responding appropriately; realizing what is behind feelings (e.g. the primary feelings underlying anger) and learning how to constructively express and control feelings.

• **Decision Making**

Examining what goes into making decisions; learning a step-by-step process for decision making; applying the process to real issues.

• **Managing Stress**

Understanding what stress is, where it comes from, and how it affects daily living; learning to use exercise, diet, guided imagery, relaxation methods, and attitude changes to control and relieve stress.

• **Personal Responsibility**

Examining actions and knowing their consequences; learning when and how to say no; recognizing the existence of personal choice in almost all situations; taking responsibility for decisions and actions.

• **Self-concept**

Establishing a firm sense of identity and feeling esteem and acceptance of oneself; monitoring "self-talk" to catch negative messages such as internal put-downs; acknowledging the talents and abilities of self and others.

• **Empathy**

Taking the perspective and understanding the feelings of others; developing caring and compassionate attitudes.

• **Communications**

Learning and practicing effective communication skills; using I-statements instead of blame; listening actively.

• **Group Dynamics**

Working self-reflectively in groups while monitoring behaviors and roles; practicing cooperation and interdependence; knowing when and how to lead and when to follow.

• **Conflict Resolution**

Understanding that conflict is normal and potentially productive; learning how to fight fair with others; learning and practicing a variety of conflict-resolution strategies, including win-win approaches to negotiating, compromise, and problem-solving.

Each of the ten units contains three group activities and two fully developed Sharing Circles, along with a list of additional Sharing Circle topics, which allow you to repeat the impact of the powerful circle process for many weeks. Before you lead your first Sharing Circle, be sure to read the section, "EQ Super Strategy: The Sharing Circle" beginning on page 19.

Many of the activities include handouts, called "Experience Sheets," for you to duplicate and distribute to students. Experience sheets are written in a conversational style and speak directly to the individual student. Directions for their use are imbedded in the printed procedure for leading each activity.

The units are arranged in a suggested order, but may be implemented with considerable flexibility. We encourage you to maintain an agile, expansive attitude as you move through (or skip among) the units. Allow the reactions of students to spark new ideas for strengthening emotional literacy skills in each topic area.

Finally, please make any adjustments necessary to accommodate the interests, abilities, cultural backgrounds and learning styles of your students. Your experience and regular contact with students put you in an ideal position to interpret signals regarding relevancy and modify the activities accordingly.

Schooling the Emotional Mind

Children have two minds — one that thinks and one that feels. An inch or so beneath the curls, buzz jobs and baseball caps, just behind the contact lenses and lashes, sit two systems operating two different yet interdependent intelligences: rational (IQ) and emotional (EQ). How children function each day and throughout life is determined by both. Rational intelligence cannot perform well without emotional intelligence, and emotional intelligence benefits from the cool cognitive judgments of the rational mind. When the two perform together smoothly and efficiently, emotional intelligence rises and so does intellectual ability.

Thanks to psychologist and author Daniel Goleman, the term *Emotional Intelligence* has become part of our daily lexicon. Goleman's best-seller *Emotional Intelligence: Why It Can Matter More Than IQ* , a superb presentation of research from education, medicine, and the behavioral and brain sciences, forms the basis for much of the ensuing discussion as well as the accompanying strategies and activities.

What Is Emotional Intelligence?

The American Heritage Dictionary defines emotion as "an intense mental state that arises subjectively rather than through conscious effort and is often accompanied by physiological changes" and as "the part of the consciousness that involves feeling; sensibility."

The word *emotion* is a derivative of the Latin root, *movere*, to move. Anyone who has experienced intense joy, desire, anger, or grief knows that emotions are anything but static mental states. Emotions are something we *do*.

Emotions shift our attention and propel us into action, rapidly organizing the responses of different biological systems — facial expression, muscle tone, voice, nerves, hormones — and putting us in optimum condition to respond. Emotions serve to establish our position relative to our environment, pulling us toward certain people, objects, actions, and ideas, and pushing us away from others. They allow us to defend ourselves in dangerous situations, fall in love, protect the things we value, mourn significant loss, and overcome difficult obstacles in the pursuit of goals.

The words *emotion* and *motivation* are closely related. In order to be strongly motivated we have to *feel* strongly. We are moved to *do* things, and we are moved *by* things. In Goleman's words, "Every strong emotion has at its root an impulse to action; managing those impulses is basic to emotional intelligence."

The terms *emotional intelligence, emotional literacy, emotional competence,* and *emotional competencies* are used in varying contexts throughout these pages. *Emotional intelligence* is the capacity to acquire and apply information of an emotional nature, to feel and to respond emotionally. This capacity resides in the emotional brain/mind. *Emotional literacy* and *emotional competence* are used interchangeably to describe the relative ability to experience and productively manage emotions. The shorthand for these terms is EQ. *Emotional competencies* are skills and attributes — self-awareness, empathy, impulse control, listening, decision making, anger management — whose level of development determines the strength of our emotional intelligence and the degree of our emotional competence.

The Sentry and the Strategist

Experts and explorers in the field of brain-based education have known or suspected for many years that emotions are the ignition switch and the octane for learning. Curriculum developers in the self-esteem arena (including this publisher) have been developing emotional intelligence under the guise of self-esteem and life-skills education for at least two decades. However, not until Goleman's book have we seen such a startling configuration of scientific evidence — case after case demonstrating the power of the emotional mind to override rational intelligence for both good and bad consequences.

The Sentry

A small structure in the limbic region of the brain, the *amygdala*, is the center of the emotional mind. All incoming data to the brain pass through the amygdala where they are instantly analyzed for their emotional value before going to the cerebral cortex for processing. Data leaving the amygdala carry an emotional charge, which, if sufficiently powerful, can override reasoned thinking and logic.

The amygdala is the specialist in emotional matters, the storehouse of emotional memory, and the seat of passion. The amygdala allows us to recognize the *personal significance* of daily events, which in turn provoke pleasure, stir compassion, arouse excitement, and incite rage.

The amygdala plays the role of sentry, scanning every incident for signs of trouble. Far quicker than the rational mind, it charges into action without regard for the consequences.

In an emotional emergency, the amygdala proclaims a crisis, recruiting the rest of the brain to its urgent agenda. Goleman calls this an *emotional hijacking*, because it occurs instantaneously, moments before the thinking brain has had a chance to grasp what is occurring and decide on the best coarse of action.

Emptying the mailbox at the end of her driveway, Marci senses a blur of movement across the street and looks up to see an elderly woman stumbling to the ground. A man is sprinting down the sidewalk with something dangling from his hand. Mail scattering in her wake, Marci flies across the street and after the man, screaming "Drop it," "Drop it." A purse bounces from the sidewalk to the gutter. Marci sees it but continues running, finally slowing to a jog as the snatcher disappears over a fence.

This is an example of an emotional hijacking. What Marci did wasn't rational. She neither witnessed a crime nor checked with the assumed victim; she didn't even see the purse until it hit the ground. Marci's emotional mind spliced together a few visual cues and produced a small feat of heroism which she had no opportunity to evaluate until it was over. What Marci felt as she jogged back to sooth her elderly neighbor, was an abating storm of outrage. Marci's own purse had been stolen a few months earlier.

In moments of crisis or intense passion, such as Marci's, the habits of the emotional brain dominate, for better or for worse. That is why, after an emotional hijacking, we express surprise at our own behavior. "I probably shouldn't have done that. I don't know what came over me," was Marci's rational evaluation moments after she returned the purse and reflected on her behavior.

The warp speed responses of the emotional mind take place without entering conscious awareness. Their purpose is to protect us from danger — to keep us alive. Our earliest ancestors needed these split-second reactions in situations where decisions had to be made instantly. Run or fight. Hide or attack. Actions that spring from the emotional mind have been measured at a few thousandths of a second and carry an overwhelming sense of certainty.

The Strategist

The critical networks on which emotion and feeling rely include not only the limbic system (amygdala), but also the neocortex — specifically the prefrontal lobes, just behind the forehead. This part of the emotional brain is able to *control* feelings in order to reappraise situations and deal with them more effectively. It functions like the control room for planning and organizing actions toward a goal. When an emotion triggers, within moments the prefrontal lobes analyze possible actions and choose the best alternative.

In the wake of intense fear or anger, for example, the neocortex is capable of producing a calmer, more appropriate response. It can even muffle emergency signals sent out by the amygdala. However, this mechanism is slower, involving more circuitry.

In Marci's case, control came too late. It isn't that she threw caution to the winds. Her own safety did not become a consideration until after the chase was over.

Internal Battles

So far, the amygdala and neocortex sound like perfect partners, the alert sentry signaling danger and the cool strategist selecting prudent courses of action. But the sentry can easily overreact, and powerful emotions can disrupt our ability to think and reason. Fear can render us mute or maniacal; anger can make us lash out visciously.

In such moments, the circuits from the amygdala to the prefrontal lobes are creating neural static, sabotaging the ability of the prefrontal lobe to maintain working memory. That's why we complain that we "can't think straight" when we are upset.

These emotional circuits, and the automatic reactions they convey, are sculpted by experience throughout childhood. Emotionally-driven automatic responses are usually learned very early — as early as four years of age. According to Goleman, all it takes is for some feature of the present situation to resemble a situation from the past. The instant that feature is recognized by the emotional mind, the feelings that went with the past event are triggered. *The emotional mind reacts to the present as if it were the past.* The reaction is fast and automatic, but not necessarily accurate or appropriate to the situation at hand. Frequently we don't even realize what is happening. Goleman describes it like this:

The emotional mind uses associative logic. It takes elements that symbolize reality or trigger a memory of it to be the same as reality. While the rational mind makes logical connections between causes and effects, the emotional mind connects things that have similar, striking features. The rational mind reasons with objective evidence; the emotional mind takes its beliefs to be absolutely true and discounts evidence to the contrary. That's why it's futile to try to reason with someone who is emotionally upset. Reasoning is out of place and carries no weight. Feelings are self-justifying.

The Impact of Emotional Intelligence

Emotions impact every area of life: health, learning, behavior, and relationships.

Children and young people who are emotionally competent— who manage their own feelings well, and who recognize and respond effectively to the feelings of others — are at an advantage in every area of life, whether family and peer relationships, school, sports, or community and organizational pursuits. Children with well-developed emotional skills are also more likely to lead happy and productive lives, and to master the habits of mind that will assure them personal and career success as adults.

In homes and schools where emotional intelligence is nurtured with the same concern as IQ, children tolerate frustration better, get into fewer fights, and engage in less self-destructive behavior. They are healthier, less lonely, less impulsive, and more focused. Human relationships improve, and so does academic achievement.

Health

There is no longer any question that emotions can profoundly affect health. Science used to believe that the brain and nervous system were separate and distinct from the immune system. In fact, the two systems are in close communication, sending messages back and forth continuously. Furthermore, chemical messengers which operate in both the brain and the immune system are concentrated *most heavily* in neural areas that regulate emotion. Here are just a few of the implications:

- Inhibiting or constraining emotions compromises immune function. People who hide their feelings or refuse to talk about significant emotional upsets are at higher risk for a variety of health problems.

- Anger, and other negative emotions are toxic to the body and pose dangers comparable to smoking cigarettes.

- Studies have linked the colds and upper respiratory infections to emotional upsets that occurred three to four days prior to the onset of symptoms.

- Numerous studies have shown that positive, supportive relationships are good medicine, bolstering immune function, speeding recovery time, and prolonging life. The prognosis for people in ill health who have caring family and friends is dramatically better than for people without emotional support.

Learning

Almost all students who do poorly in school lack one or more elements of emotional intelligence. Study after study has shown that competence in emotional skills results not only in higher academic achievement on the part of students, but in significantly more instructional time on the part of teachers. Emotionally competent children are far less disruptive and require fewer disciplinary interventions.

Furthermore, academic intelligence, as measured by IQ and SAT scores, is not a reliable predictor of who will succeed in life. IQ contributes about 20 percent to factors that determine life success, which leaves 80 percent to other forces. Numerous studies have shown that IQ has minimal impact on how individuals lead their lives — how happy they are, and how successful. One major reason is that while cognitive skills are tied to IQ, desire and motivation are products of emotional intelligence. Children who are emotionally competent have an increased desire to learn and to achieve, both within school and without. Positive emotions — excitement, curiosity, pride — are the fuel that drives motivation. Passion moves young people toward their goals.

Behavior

Violence and disorder in America's schools have reached crisis proportions. Teachers who once dealt with mischievous, unruly students and an occasional temper tantrum are now demanding emergency phones in their classrooms, security guards in the hallways, and metal detectors at the gates. As long as such conditions continue, all education suffers. Rates of teen suicide, pregnancy, and drug abuse testify to the need for emotional literacy: self-awareness, decision-making, self-confidence, and stress management.

Relationships

Children who are effective in social interactions are capable of understanding their peers. They know how to interact with other children and adults — flexibly, skillfully, and responsibly — without sacrificing their own needs and integrity. They have a good sense of timing and are effective at being heard and getting help when they need it. Socially competent children can process the nonverbal as well as verbal messages of others, and recognize that the behaviors of one person can affect another. They take responsibility for their actions.

Children who cannot interpret or express emotions feel frustrated. They don't understand what's going on around them. They are frequently viewed as strange, and cause others to feel uncomfortable. Without social competence, children can easily misinterpret a look or statement and respond inappropriately, yet lack the ability to express their uncertainty or clarify the intentions and desires of others. They may lack empathy and be relatively unaware of how their behavior affects others.

Early Development

The first school for emotional literacy is the home. How parents treat their children has deep and lasting consequences for their emotional life.

In order to help children deal constructively with their emotions, parents must themselves have a reasonable degree of emotional literacy. The children of emotionally competent parents handle their own emotions better, are more adept at soothing themselves when they are upset, enjoy better physical health, are better liked by their peers, are more socially skilled, have fewer behavior problems, greater attention spans, and score higher on achievement tests.

Parents who ignore or show a lack of respect for their child's feelings, or who accept any emotional response as appropriate, are putting their child in peril not only for emotional development, but for intellectual development as well.

Bullies — children who tend toward violence — have parents who ignore them most of the time, show little interest in their lives, yet punish them severely for real or perceived transgressions. These parents are not necessarily mean-spirited, they are usually repeating parenting styles that were practiced on them in childhood. Intellectually, they may want the best for their children, but have no inkling how to achieve it.

The emotional skill that violent children lack above all others is empathy. They are unable to feel what their victim is feeling, to view the situation through the eyes of the other child. In many cases, this lack of empathy is due to parental abuse. Abuse kills empathy.

Children who are repeatedly abused often suffer from post-traumatic stress disorder (PTSD). When a child's life is in danger and there is nothing the child can do to escape the peril, the brain actually changes.

A structure within the brain of children with PTSD secrets extra-large doses of brain chemicals in response to situations that are reminders of traumatic events, even when present events hold little or no threat. Oversecretions also occur from the pituitary gland, which alerts the body to danger and stimulates the fight or flight response. Thus, PTSD is a *limbic disorder.*

The good news is that the behavior of emotionally troubled children — bullies and children with PTSD — can change. The emotional circuitry can be rewired through relearning.

Emotional Windows

Research indicates that being bold or shy, upbeat or melancholy is at least partially genetic. Children may be predisposed to a certain temperament based on the relative excitability of the amygdala. However these innate emotional patterns can be improved with the right experiences.

Early emotional learning poses a similar problem. Synaptic connections are formed very quickly, in a matter of hours or days. In Goleman's words, "Experience, particularly in childhood, sculpts the brain."

The key skills of emotional intelligence each have a critical learning period extending over several years in childhood. Massive sculpting of neural circuits takes place during these periods, each of which represents an optimal "emotional window" for learning specific skills. Once the emotional brain learns something, it never lets it go; once a window is closed, the pathway is forever etched. That's why changing in adulthood is so difficult. In fact, the patterns probably never change, though they can be controlled through new insights and with new learned responses.

The responses of the amygdala are well established long before a child leaves elementary school; however, the frontal lobes which regulate the limbic impulse mature into adolescence. Through skills and habits acquired at later ages, children can still learn to control their feelings, turn down the emotional thermostat, and substitute positive behaviors for negative.

Gender Differences

Girls receive significantly more education regarding emotions from their parents than do boys. In discussion, play, and fantasy, mothers cover a wider range of emotions with their daughters than with their sons.

Combine this greater knowledge with the fact that girls develop language skills more quickly than do boys and it is clear why girls find it easier to articulate their feelings and to use verbal exploration of feelings as substitutes for physical confrontations and fights, a difference that behavioral scientists have measured at about age 13. The chart summarizes gender differences in emotional intelligence.

Girls at 13:	Boys at 13:
• are adept at reading verbal and nonverbal emotional signals and expressing feelings.	• are adept at expressing anger
• experience a wide range of emotions with intensity and volatility.	• minimize emotions having to do with vulnerability, guilt, fear, and hurt.
• have learned to use tactics like ostracism, gossip, and indirect vendettas as substitutes for aggression.	• are confrontational when angry
• see themselves as part of a web of connectedness.	• take pride in a lone, tough-minded independence and autonomy

Controlling Emotions

If the sentry (the amygdala) and the neural pathways can't be changed, then the primary goal of emotional education is to improve the skills of the strategist — the neocortex. As we've seen, the neocortex is capable of managing the amygdala by reshaping its responses. Children will still have their emotional outbursts, but can learn to control how long they last and the behaviors they produce.

Psychotherapy is a classic example of this process, with the client engaging in systematic emotional relearning. Therapy teaches people to control their emotional responses. Consistent positive discipline — the kind that focuses on feelings underlying behavior and on identifying alternatives to unacceptable behavior — accomplishes the same thing.

The ability to bring out-of-control emotions back into line results in what our parents and grandparents called *emotional maturity.* Present terminology labels it *emotional competence,* the "master aptitude."

Self-Awareness

The first step in getting children to control their emotional responses is to help them develop self-awareness. Through self-awareness, children learn to give ongoing attention to their internal states, to know what they are feeling when they are feeling it, to identify the events that precipitate upsets and emotional hijackings, and to bring their feelings back under control. Goleman defines self-awareness as:

...awareness of a feeling or mood and our thoughts about the feeling. ...a slight stepping-back from experience, a parallel stream of consciousness that is "meta": hovering above or beside the main flow, aware of what is happening rather than being immersed and lost in it.

Self-awareness allows children to manage their feelings and to recover from bad moods more quickly. Children who are self-aware don't hide things from themselves. Labeling feelings makes them their own. They can talk about fear, frustration, excitement, and envy and they can understand and speculate concerning such feelings in others, too.

Lacking self-awareness, children may become engulfed by their feelings, lost in them, overwhelmed by them. Unawareness of what is going on in their inner and outer worlds sets the stage for lack of congruence between what they believe or feel and how they behave. Feelings of isolation ("I'm the only one who feels this way.") occur when children are unaware that others experience the same range of feelings that they do. Without self-awareness children never gain control over their lives. By default, their courses are plotted by others or by parts of themselves which they fail to recognize.

Self-awareness can take the form of nonjudgmental observation ("I'm feeling irritated.") or it can be accompanied by evaluative thoughts ("I shouldn't feel this way" or "Don't think about that.") Although in and of themselves, emotions are neither right nor wrong, good nor bad, these kinds of judgments are common and indicate that the neocortical circuits are monitoring the emotion. However, to try to abolish a feeling or attempt to take away a feeling in someone else only drives the emotion out of awareness, where its activity along neural pathways continues unmonitored and unabated — as neuroses, insomnia, ulcers, and communication failures of all kinds testify.

Managing Anger and Curbing Impulses

Eric started his day, not to the sounds of the birds or the local morning DJ, but to the jarring pre-dawn combat of his warring parents. The breakfast cereal was gone, the milk was sour, and there were no clean diapers for the baby whose fussing and screaming at length interrupted the din from the master bedroom. Accused of hurting the baby, Eric was scolded by his mother and slapped by his father. He fled the house without books or homework, almost missed the bus, and when he got to school was berated by his teacher for coming unprepared. At recess, Eric walked into the path of a speeding soccer ball, which stung his back and knocked him breathless. When he regained his wind, Eric found the boy who had kicked the ball and beat him until his face was bloody.

Eric had plenty of reasons to be angry. What he did not have, at least in this incident, were the internal skills or the external support system to help him process his feelings and prevent the anger from building.

Threats to life, security, and self-esteem trigger a two-part limbic surge: First, hormones called *catecholamines* are released, generating a rush of energy that lasts for minutes. Second, an adrenocortical arousal is created that can put a child on edge and keep him there for hours, sometimes days. This explains why children (including Eric) are more likely to erupt in anger over something relatively innocuous if the incident is preceded by an earlier upsetting experience. Though the two events may be completely unrelated, the anger generated by the second incident builds on the anger left over from the first. Irritation turns to anger, anger to rage, and rage erupts in violence.

Contrary to what many of us used to believe, when it comes to anger "letting it all out" is *not* helpful. Acting on anger will generally make a child angrier, and each angry outburst will prolong and deepen the distress.

What does work is to teach children to keep a lid on their feelings while they buy some time. If children wait until they have cooled down, they can confront the other person calmly. When flooded with negative emotions the ability to hear, think, and speak are severely impaired. Taking a "time out" can be enormously constructive. However 5 minutes is not enough; research suggests that people need at least 20 minutes to recover from intense physiological arousal.

Research has also shown quite conclusively that it's possible for a child to keep an angry mood going (and growing) just by thinking (and talking) about it.

> *Remembered or imagined experiences can create the same flood of chemistry as the experience itself*
> —Ellen Langer
> Harvard University, 1986

> *Thinking about a stressful situation produces the same bodily and mental responses as the experience itelf.*
> —American Medical Association
> Annual Research Conference, 1993

The longer a child dwells on what made her angry, the more reasons and self-justifications she can find for being angry. So when encouraging children to talk about their feelings, we need to be careful not to fan the flames.

Brooding fuels anger, but seeing things differently quells it. Reframing a situation is one of the most potent ways of controlling emotions.

Sadness: Shifting Gears

Depression and sadness are low-arousal states. When a child is sad, it's as though a master gauge has turned down everything: mouth, eyes, head, shoulders, speech, energy, motivation, desire. Taking a jog is probably the last thing the child feels like doing, but by forcing himself out the door and down the path, he will experience a lift.

The key seems to be shifting the mind from a low-arousal state to a high-arousal state. Exercise and positive distracting activities, like seeing a funny movie, turn up the master gauge, relieving sadness, melancholy, and mild depression. Another way to accomplish the shift is to engineer a small success, such as improving a skill, winning a game, or completing a project.

Humor is great at lifting children out of the doldrums and can add significantly to their creativity and ability to solve problems, too. In studies documenting the effects of humor, people were able to think more broadly, associate more freely, and generate more creative solutions and decisions after hearing a joke.

The ability of humor to boost creativity and improve decision making stems from the fact that memory is "state specific." When we're in a good mood, we come up with more positive solutions and decisions. When we're in a bad mood, the alternatives we generate reflect our negativity.

Choosing to watch cartoons, shoot baskets, ride a bike, or spend a few minutes on the computer is a decision that takes place in the neocortex. The amygdala can't be stopped from generating sadness and melancholy, but children can teach their neocortex a way out of the gloom.

Relationship Skills

If they are fortunate, children are surrounded by people who give them attention, are actively involved in their lives, and model healthy, responsible interpersonal behavior. Core skills in the art of relationships are empathy, listening, mastery of nonverbal cues, and the ability to manage the emotions of others — to make accurate interpretations, respond appropriately, work cooperatively, and resolve conflicts.

Howard Gardner's theory of multiplicity intelligence includes two personal intelligences, *interpersonal* and *intrapersonal.* People with high interpersonal intelligence have the capacity to discern and respond appropriately to the moods, temperaments, motivations, and desires of others. Intrapersonal intelligence gives people ready access to their own feeling life, the ability to discriminate among their emotions, and accurate awareness of their strengths and weaknesses.

The personal intelligences equip children to monitor their own expressions of emotion, attune to the ways others react, fine-tune their social performance to have the desired effect, express unspoken collective sentiments and guide groups toward goals. Personal intelligence is the basis of leadership.

Lacking personal intelligence, young people are apt to make poor choices related to such important decisions as who to befriend, emulate, date, and marry, what skills to develop and what career to pursue.

Components of Interpersonal Intelligence

- **Organizing groups:** directing, producing, leading activities and organizations

- **Negotiating solutions:** mediating, preventing and resolving conflicts, deal-making, arbitrating

- **Personal connections:** reading emotions and responding appropriately to the feelings and needs of others; teaming, cooperating

- **Social analysis:** insightful concerning the motives, concerns and feelings of others; able to size up situations

Components of Intrapersonal Intelligence

- **Self-knowledge and analysis:** having an accurate model of oneself and using that model to operate effectively in life; understanding own values, attitudes, habits, belief systems, strengths, weaknesses, and the motives that drive actions

- **Access to feelings:** the ability to discriminate among feelings and draw upon them to guide behavior; to identify and respond appropriately to own emotions

- **Personal organization:** the ability to clarify goals, plan, motivate, and follow through

- **Impulse control:** the ability to delay gratification; to deny impulse in the service of a goal

- **Fantasy and creativity:** the ability to nuture a rich and rewarding inner life

Empathy. All social skills are built on a base of emotional attunement, on the capacity for empathy. The ability to "walk in another's moccasins" is the foundation of caring and altruism. Violent people lack empathy.

Empathy is an outgrowth of self-awareness. The more we are able to understand our own emotions, the more skilled we are at understanding and responding to the emotions of others. Empathy plays heavily in making moral judgments. Sharing their pain, fear, or neglect is what moves us to help people in distress. Putting ourselves in the place of others motivates us to follow moral principles — to treat others the way we want to be treated.

These abilities have little to do with rational intelligence. Studies have shown that students with high levels of empathy are among the most popular, well adjusted, and high performing students, yet their IQs are no higher than those of students who are less skilled at reading nonverbal cues.

Empathy begins to develop very early in life. When infants and children under two witness the upset of another child, they react as if the distress were their own. Seeing another child cry is likely to bring them to tears and send them to a parent's arms.

From about the age of two on, when children begin to grasp the concept of their own separateness, they typically seek to console a distressed child by giving toys, petting, or hugging. In late childhood, they are able to view distress as an outgrowth of a person's condition or station in life. At this stage of development, children are capable of empathizing with entire groups such as the poor, the homeless, and victims of war.

Empathy can be developed through various forms of perspective-taking. In conflict situations, children can be asked to listen to each other's feelings and point of view, and then to feed back or summarize the opposing perspective. Imagining the feelings of characters in literature as well as figures from current events and history is also effective. Combining role playing with these strategies makes them even more powerful.

Nonverbal Communication Skills. The mode of communication used by the rational mind is words; the mode preferred by the emotional mind is nonverbal. We telegraph and receive excitement, happiness, sorrow, anger, and all the other emotions through facial expressions and body movements. When words contradict these nonverbal messages — "I'm fine," hissed through clenched teeth — nine times out of ten we can believe the nonverbal and discount the verbal.

Acting out various feelings teaches children to be more aware of nonverbal behavior, as does identifying feelings from videos, photos, and illustrations.

Emotions are contagious and transferrable. When two children interact, the more emotionally expressive of the pair readily transfers feelings to the more passive. Again, this transfer is accomplished *nonverbally.*

Children with high levels of emotional intelligence are able to attune to other children's (and adult's) moods and bring others under the sway of their own feelings, setting the emotional tone of an interaction.

Guided by cultural background, children learn certain display rules concerning the expression of emotions, such as minimizing or exaggerating particular feelings, or substituting one feeling for another, as when a child displays confidence while feeling confused. As educators in a multiethnic, multiracial society, we need to be sensitive to a variety of cultural display rules, and help students gain a similar awareness.

Listening. Through listening, children learn empathy, gather information, develop cooperative relationships, and build trust. Skillful listening is required for engaging in conversations and discussions, negotiating agreements, resolving conflicts and many other emotional and cognitive competencies.

Few skills have greater and more lasting value than listening. Unfortunately, listening skills are generally learned by happenstance, not by direct effort. The vast majority of children and adults are either unable or unwilling to listen attentively and at length to another person.

Research shows that poor listening impedes learning and destroys comprehension. However, when students are taught to listen effectively, both comprehension and academic performance go up, along with classroom cooperation and self-esteem. Listening facilitates both emotional learning and relearning — strengthening and refining the analytical and corrective functions of the neocortex.

Conflict Management. Schools are rife with opportunities for conflict. From the farthest reaches of the playground to the most remote corners of the classroom, from student restrooms to the teacher's lounge, a thousand little things each day create discord. The causes are many.

Children bring to school an accumulation of everything they've learned — all of their habits and all the beliefs they've developed about themselves, other people, and their world. Such diversity makes conflict inevitable. And because the conflict-resolution skills of most children are poorly developed, the outcomes of conflict are frequently negative — at times even destructive.

Diversity also breeds conflict. Learning to understand, respect and appreciate similarities and differences is one key to resolving conflicts. Unfortunately most of us learn as children that there is only one right answer. From the moment this fallacious notion receives acceptance, the mind closes and vision narrows.

Prejudice cannot be eliminated, but the emotional learning underlying prejudice can be *relearned*. One way to accomplish relearning is to engineer projects and activities in which diverse groups work together to obtain common goals. Social cliques, particularly hostile ones, intensify negative stereotypes. But when children work together as equals to attain a common goal — on committees, sports teams, performing groups — stereotypes break down.

Peer mediation programs offer another excellent avenue for relearning ineffective emotional responses to conflict. Mediators act as models, facilitators and coaches, helping their classmates develop listening, conflict resolution, and problem-solving skills.

Educating the Emotional Brain

Emotional intelligence is a core competence. To raise the level of social and emotional skills in students, schools need to focus on the emotional aspects of children's lives, which most currently ignore.

Unfortunately, in classes that stress subject-matter mastery, teaching is often devoid of emotional content. Too many educators believe that if somehow students master school subjects, they will be well prepared for life. Such a view suffers from a shallow and distorted understanding of how the human brain functions.

Joan Caulfield and Wayne Jennings, experts in brain-based education, specify four building blocks for incorporating emotional intelligence concepts in schools:

1. Safety, security, unconditional love and nurturing for every child

2. Stimulating classroom environments which provide rich sensory input to the brain

3. Experiential learning; opportunities to engage skills, knowledge and attitudes in a wide variety of real life tests

4. Useful and timely performance feedback

Many of the competencies that should be addressed by educational programs in emotional literacy have been specified on the previous pages. A number of outlines are suggested by Goleman in his book, *Emotional Intelligence*. One of the most useful comes from Peter Salovey, a Yale psychologist whose list of emotional competencies includes five domains and incorporates Howard Gardner's theories on interpersonal and intrapersonal intelligences.

1. **Knowing one's emotions:** Self awareness — recognizing a feeling as it happens. Monitoring feelings from moment to moment

2. **Managing emotions:** Emotional competence. Handling feelings; ability to recover quickly from upsets and distress;

3. **Motivating oneself:** Marshaling emotions in order to reach goals; self-control and self-discipline; delaying gratification and stifling impulsiveness

4. **Recognizing emotions in others:** Empathy — the ability to recognize, identify, and feel what another is feeling.

5. **Handling relationships:** The ability to manage emotions in others; social competence; leadership skills

To be most effective, emotional literacy content and processes should be applied consistently across the curriculum and at all grade levels. Children should be afforded many opportunities for skill practice, through a combination of dedicated activities and the countless unplanned "teachable moments" that occur daily. When emotional lessons are repeated over and over, they are reflected in strengthened neural pathways in the brain. They become positive habits that surface in times of stress.

Weaving EQ Into the Curriculum

Teachers may resist the idea of adding new content areas to the curriculum. In most cases, demands on teacher time are already at or beyond the saturation point, but this needn't be an insurmountable obstacle to emotional education. Feelings are part of everything that children do, and they can be part of everything they learn, too.

By incorporating lessons in emotional intelligence within traditional subject areas, we assist students to grasp the connections between realms of academic knowledge and life experience, and encourage them to utilize their multiple intelligences. This approach fits well with the concept of multidisciplinary teaching.

When a curriculum adheres to traditional straight and narrow subject areas and is devoid of emotional content, the subject matter is unlikely to "live" for students because of the curriculum's cold and reductionistic nature. With the world growing more complex by the minute, such an approach makes it extremely difficult for children to integrate the parts and pieces of what they learn, much less apply them within a real-world context.

By suggesting relationships and posing the right questions, by being observant and noticing nonverbal signals, teachers can help to surface and deal with emotional elements in every lesson, no matter what the subject area. Likewise they can take moments of personal crisis and turn them into lessons in emotional competence.

The Facilitator Role

Some teachers gravitate toward lessons in emotional intelligence and need little encouragement; if you are one of those, great! However, if you are uncomfortable talking about feelings, consider enlisting the help of the school counselor. Very little in traditional teacher education prepared you for this role, so start slowly and concentrate on becoming an effective facilitator of emotional inquiry. Here are just a few suggestions:

1. Rethink (and help colleagues, administrators, and parents rethink) traditional approaches to discipline. Substitute skill development for punishment, using misbehavior, upsets, and fighting as opportunities to teach children impulse control, conflict management, perspective taking, and awareness of feelings.

2. Strike a cooperative agreement with your school counselor. Invite the counselor to visit the classroom to lead emotional literacy activities.

3. Conduct class meetings to deal with issues and problems that the students submit for discussion. Create and decorate an "emotional mailbox" for the classroom, and encourage students to submit questions and problem descriptions.

4. Identify the dominant learning styles of individual students as a way of facilitating "flow." Flow is what we experience when we are so completely absorbed in a task or project that progress is effortless.

   In a state of flow, a child is completely relaxed yet intensely focused. Minimal mental energy is expended. Flow is characterized by an absence of limbic static and superfluous brain activity; emotions are positive and totally aligned with the task at hand.

An excellent way to encourage flow is to apply Gardner's theory of multiple intelligences, thus assuring that students engage in processes that are right for them and that utilize their competencies, learning styles, and talents. This allows the teacher to play to the strengths of children while attempting to shore up areas of weakness. As Goleman argues: "Pursuing flow through learning is a more humane, natural, and very likely more effective way to marshal emotions in the service of education."

5. Use cooperative learning principles and strategies. Cooperative learning optimizes the acquisition of subject-area knowledge while developing skills and concepts beyond those afforded by isolated study. Cooperation and collaboration mean that more information is discovered, processed, shared, and applied. And the fact that students process the information and find solutions along with their peers results in the development of a host of interpersonal and social skills.

By participating in team activities, students learn important lessons about group dynamics and develop extremely valuable communication skills. As students assimilate content, participating in team projects teaches them the value and skills of trust building, listening, respecting others' points of view, articulating ideas, planning, making choices, dividing the labor, encouraging others, taking responsibility, solving problems, compromising, managing and resolving conflicts, and celebrating team successes, to name just some of the benefits.

6. In addition to the emotional literacy activities in this book, be prepared for daily impromptu facilitation of emotional learning. For example:

- At a learning center, keep a doll-house replica of the classroom with a stick figure representing each student and the teacher. Allow the students to take turns pairing and teaming the figures to show who plays and works with whom, close friendships, antagonistic relationships, and where in the room individual students prefer to work. Use the same materials to reenact real conflicts that occur in the classroom.

- Order a video that shows a variety of emotions displayed via facial expressions or body movements. If a video is out of the question, collect photos from magazines. Have the students practice identifying the emotions from the nonverbal cues. Then invite them to act out the same emotions themselves.

- Work with children to bolster their sense of agency relative to the ups and downs in their lives. If a child shows signs of early depression, enlist the help of the school counselor. Children who are candidates for depression seem to believe that bad things (for example, a low grade) happen to them because of some inherent flaw ("I'm stupid"), and that there is nothing they can do to change these conditions. More optimistic children look for solutions, such as increased study time.

- Teach and counsel children to control anger in these ways:

—Change the thoughts that trigger anger, reassessing the situation with a different (less provocative) point of view. Often this involves looking at the situation from the other person's perspective. "Perhaps Sue is having a bad day." "Maybe Juan doesn't feel well." Changing thoughts produces new feelings which displace the anger.

—Cool off through active exercise or distracting activities.

—Write down angry thoughts and then challenge and reappraise them.

—Identify and express the feelings that precede anger. Anger is often a secondary emotion, erupting in the wake of other feelings, like frustration, fear, or humiliation.

—Monitor the feelings and bodily sensations they experience when they're becoming angry. Learn to use these sensations as cues to stop and consider what is happening and what to do about it.

Organizational EQ

Let's take a minute to talk about ourselves — our own emotional intelligence, and the modeling we do for children. After all, educators have feelings, too.

Almost every organization, educational and otherwise, harbors a vast emotional undercurrent, a shadowy hidden world of unexpressed feeling. While on the surface we may appear calm and rational, underneath we are churning with emotions: resentment, jealousy, love, fear, guilt, revulsion, caring, pride, frustration, confusion, and joy.

We spend untold time and energy protecting ourselves from people we don't trust, avoiding problems we're afraid to broach, tiptoeing around performance issues, pretending to accept decisions with which we disagree, accepting jobs and assignments we don't want, and withholding our opinions and insights. What a waste. Emotions can help solve problems. Let's use them.

Emotional energy, whether positive or negative, moves us to action. Emotions are the source of passion, motivation, and commitment. When we share our feelings and opinions, work and work relationships are experienced as more vital and meaningful, and movement toward goals accelerates.

We must do everything we can to build schools where feelings are recognized, communication flows freely, and conflicts are handled productively. Where we can air complaints honestly, knowing that they will be viewed as helpful, where diversity is valued and nourished, and inclusion and interdependence are experienced at many levels.

The brightest futures belong to students who develop EQ along with IQ, and to school communities whose citizens have the courage to risk being human in the classroom, lunchroom, office, playground, workroom, and playing field.

When we *model* emotional intelligence, we employ the most potent teaching strategy of all.

EQ Super Strategy: The Sharing Circle

To achieve its goals, *50 Activities for Teaching Emotional Intelligence* incorporates a variety of proven instructional strategies. Activities include simulations, role plays, "experience sheets" for individual students to complete, and a host of small and large group experiments and discussions.

One of the most powerful and versatile of the instructional strategies used in this curriculum is the Sharing Circle. In each unit, two Sharing Circles are fully elaborated. These are followed by a list of additional Sharing Circle topics relevant to the unit topic. At first glance, the Sharing Circle — a small-group discussion process — is likely to appear deceptively simple. It is not. When used correctly, the Sharing Circle is unusually effective as a tool for developing self-awareness, the ability to understand and manage feelings, self-concept, personal responsibility, empathy, communication and group interaction skills.

The Sharing Circle is an ideal way to incorporate emotional learning in the classroom on a regular basis, and helps to form the four building blocks suggested by brain-based education experts Joan Caulfield and Wayne Jennings (see page 14). First, the Sharing Circle provides safety, security, unconditional love and nurturing to each child. Second, Sharing Circle structure and procedures constitute a marked departure from traditional classroom teaching/learning approaches. Topics are stimulating in their ability to provoke self-inquiry. The ambiance is close yet respectful, over time causing intrapersonal defenses and interpersonal barriers to shrink and leading to new levels of group cohesiveness and creativity. Third, circle topics address real-life experiences and issues and the full range of emotions associated with them. And finally, the immediacy of the circle ensures that every child's contributions are heard and accepted on the spot. The attentiveness of other circle members along with their verbal and nonverbal emotional and cognitive reactions constitute a legitimate and powerful form of affirming feedback.

Please take the time to read the following sections before leading your first circle. Once you are familiar with the process, implement Sharing Circles regularly and as frequently as you can.

An Overview of the Sharing Circle

Twenty-seven years of teaching the Sharing Circle process to educators world wide have demonstrated the power of the Sharing Circle in contributing to the development of emotional intelligence. To take full advantage of this process there are some things you need to know.

First, the topic elaboration provided under the heading, "Introduce the Topic," in each Sharing Circle is intended as a guide and does not have to be read verbatim. Once you have used Sharing Circles for a while and are feeling comfortable with the process, you will undoubtedly want to substitute your own words of introduction. We are merely providing you with ideas.

In your elaboration, try to use language and examples that are appropriate to the age, ability, and culture of your students. In our examples, we have attempted to be as general as possible; however, those examples may not be the most appropriate for your students.

Second, we strongly urge you to respect the integrity of the sharing and discussion phases of the circle. These two phases are procedurally and qualitatively different, yet of equal importance in promoting awareness, insight, and higher-level thinking in students. The longer you lead Sharing Circles, the more you will appreciate the instructional advantages of maintaining this unique relationship.

All Sharing Circle topics are intended to develop awareness and insight through voluntary sharing. The discussion questions allow students to understand what has been shared at deeper levels, to evaluate ideas that have been generated by the topic, and to apply specific concepts to other areas of learning.

In order for students to lead fulfilling, productive lives, to interact effectively with others, and to become adept at understanding and responding appropriately to the emotions of others, they first need to become aware of themselves and their own emotions. They need to know who they are, how they feel and function, and how they relate to others.

When used regularly, the *process* of the Sharing Circle coupled with its *content* (specific discussion topics) provides students with frequent opportunities to become more aware of their strengths, abilities, and positive qualities. In the Sharing Circle, students are listened to when they express their feelings and ideas, and they learn to listen to each other. The Sharing Circle format provides a framework in which genuine attention and acceptance can be given and received on a consistent basis.

By sharing their experiences and feelings in a safe environment, students are able to see basic commonalties among human beings — and individual differences, too. This understanding contributes to the development of self-respect. On a foundation of self-respect, students grow to understand and respect others.

As an instructional tool, the purpose of the Sharing Circle is to promote growth and development in students of all ages. Targeted growth areas include communication, self-awareness, personal mastery, and interpersonal skills. As students follow the rules and relate to each other verbally during the Sharing Circle,

they are practicing oral communication and learning to listen. Through insights developed in the course of pondering and discussing the various topics, students are offered the opportunity to grow in awareness and to feel more masterful — more in control of their feelings, thoughts, and behaviors. Through the positive experience of give and take, they learn more about effective modes of social interaction.

The Value of Listening

Many of us do not realize that merely listening to students talk can be immensely facilitating to their personal development. We do not need to diagnose, probe, or problem solve to help students focus attention on their own needs and use the information and insights in their own minds to arrive at their own conclusions. Because being listened to gives students confidence in their ability to positively affect their own lives, listening is certainly the facilitative method with the greatest long-term payoff.

When a student is dealing with a problem, or when her emotional state clearly indicates that something is bothering her, active listening is irreplaceable as a means of helping.

The Sharing Circle provides the opportunity for students to talk while others actively listen. By being given this opportunity, students gain important self-knowledge. Once they see that we do not intend to change them and that they may speak freely without threat of being "wrong," students find it easier to examine themselves and begin to see areas where they can make positive change in their lives. Just through the consistent process of sharing in a safe environment, students develop the ability to clarify their feelings and thoughts. They are encouraged to go deeper, find their own direction, and express and face strong feelings that may at other times be hidden obstacles to their growth. The important point is that students really can solve their own problems, develop self-awareness, and learn skills that will enable them to become responsible members of society if they are listened to effectively.

Awareness

Words are the only tool we have for systematically turning our attention and awareness to the feelings within us, and for describing and reflecting on our thoughts and behaviors. Feelings, after all, lead people to marry, to seek revenge, to launch war, to create great works of art, and to commit their lives to the service of others. They are vital and compelling.

For students to be able to manage their feelings, they must know what those feelings are. To know what they are, they must practice describing them in words. When a particular feeling is grasped in words several times, the mind soon begins to automatically recall ideas and concepts in association with the feeling and can start to provide ways of dealing with the feeling; e.g., "I'm feeling angry and I need to get away from this situation to calm down."

With practice, the mind becomes more and more adept at making these connections. When a recognized feeling comes up, the mind can sort through alternative responses to the feeling. As a student practices this response sequence in reaction to a variety of feelings, he will find words floating into consciousness that accurately identify what is going on emotionally and physically for him. This knowledge in turn develops the capacity to think before and during action. One mark of high emotional intelligence is the ability to recognize one's feelings and to take appropriate, responsible action. The lower a student's EQ, the more often emotional hijackings will determine her behavior. The ability to put words to feelings, to understand those words, to sort through an internal repertoire of responses and to choose appropriate, responsible behavior in reaction to a feeling indicates a high level of self-awareness and emotional intelligence.

By verbally exploring their own experiences in the circle and listening to others do the same, all in an environment of safety, students are gently and gradually prompted to explore deeper within themselves and to grow and expand in their understanding of others. As this mutual sharing takes place, they learn that feelings, thoughts, and behaviors are real and experienced by everyone. They see others succeeding and failing in the same kinds of ways they succeed and fail. They also begin to see each person as unique and to realize that they are unique, too. Out of this understanding, students experience a growing concern for others. A sense of responsibility develops as the needs, problems, values, and preferences of others penetrate their awareness.

Personal Mastery

Personal mastery can be defined as self-confidence together with responsible competence. Self-confidence is believing in oneself as a capable human being. Responsible competence is the willingness to take responsibility for one's actions coupled with the ability to demonstrate fundamental human relations skills (competencies).

Through participation in Sharing Circles, students are encouraged to explore their successes and hear positive comments about their efforts. Many Sharing Circle topics heighten students' awareness of their own successes and those of others. Failure, or falling short, is a reality that is also examined. The focus, however, is not to remind students that they have failed; instead these topics enable students to see that falling short is common and universal and is experienced by all people when they strive to accomplish things.

Sharing circle topics often address human relations competencies, such as the ability to include others, assume and share responsibility, offer help, behave assertively, solve problems, resolve conflicts, etc. Such topics elevate awareness in the human relations domain and encourage students to more effectively exercise these competencies and skills each day. The first step in a student's developing any competency is knowing that he or she is capable of demonstrating it. The Sharing Circle is particularly adept at helping students to recognize and acknowledge their own capabilities.

A particularly important element of personal mastery is personal responsibility. By focusing on their positive behaviors and accomplishments, the attention of students is directed toward the internal and external rewards that can be gained when they behave responsibly.

The Sharing Circle is a wonderful tool for teaching cooperation. As equitably as possible, the circle structure attempts to meet the needs of all participants. Everyone's feelings are accepted. Comparisons and judgments are not made. The circle is not another competitive arena, but is guided by a spirit of collaboration. When students practice fair, respectful interaction with one another, they benefit from the experience and are likely to employ these responsible behaviors in other life situations.

Interpersonal Skills

Relating effectively to others is a challenge we all face. People who are effective in their social interactions have the ability to understand others. They know how to interact flexibly, skillfully, and responsibly. At the same time, they recognize their own needs and maintain their own integrity. Socially effective people can process the nonverbal as well as verbal messages of others. They possess the very important awareness that all people have the power to affect one another. They are aware of not only how others affect them, but the effects their behaviors have on others.

The Sharing Circle process has been designed so that healthy, responsible behaviors are modeled by the teacher or counselor in his or her role as circle leader. The rules also require that the students relate positively and effectively to one another. The Sharing Circle brings out and affirms the positive qualities inherent in everyone and allows students to practice

effective modes of communication. Because Sharing Circles provide a place where participants are listened to and their feelings accepted, students learn how to provide the same conditions to peers and adults outside the circle.

One of the great benefits of the Sharing Circle is that it does not merely teach young people about social interaction, it lets them interact! Every Sharing Circle is a real-life experience of social interaction where the students share, listen, explore, plan, dream, and problem solve together. As they interact, they learn about each other and they realize what it takes to relate effectively to others. Any given Sharing Circle may provide a dozen tiny flashes of positive interpersonal insight for an individual participant. Gradually, the reality of what constitutes effective behavior in relating to others is internalized.

Through this regular sharing of interpersonal experiences, the students learn that behavior can be positive or negative, and sometimes both at the same time. Consequences can be constructive, destructive, or both. Different people respond differently to the same event. They have different feelings and thoughts. The students begin to understand what will cause what to happen; they grasp the concept of cause and effect; they see themselves affecting others and being affected by others.

The ability to make accurate interpretations and responses in social interactions allows students to know where they stand with themselves and with others. They can tell what actions "fit" a situation. Sharing circles are marvelous testing grounds where students can observe themselves and others in action, and can begin to see themselves as contributing to the good and bad feelings of others. With this understanding, students are helped to conclude that being responsible towards others feels good, and is the most valuable and personally rewarding form of interaction.

How to Set Up Sharing Circles

Group Size and Composition

Sharing Circles are a time for focusing on individuals' contributions in an unhurried fashion. For this reason, each circle group needs to be kept relatively small — eight to twelve usually works best. Once they move beyond the primary grades, students are capable of extensive verbalization. You will want to encourage this, and not stifle them because of time constraints.

Each group should be as heterogeneous as possible with respect to sex, ability, and racial/ethnic background. Sometimes there will be a group in which all the students are particularly reticent to speak. At these times, bring in an expressive student or two who will get things going. Sometimes it is necessary for practical reasons to change the membership of a group. Once established, however, it is advisable to keep a group as stable as possible.

Length and Location of Circles

Most circle sessions last approximately 20 to 30 minutes. At first students tend to be reluctant to express themselves fully because they do not yet know that the circle is a safe place. Consequently your first sessions may not last more than 10 to 15 minutes. Generally speaking, students become comfortable and motivated to speak with continued experience.

In middle-school classrooms circle sessions may be conducted at any time during the class period. Starting circle sessions at the beginning of the period allows additional time in case students become deeply involved in the topic. If you start circles late in the period, make sure the students are aware of their responsibility to be concise.

In elementary classes, any time of day is appropriate for Sharing Circles. Some teachers like to set the tone for the day by beginning with circles; others feel it's a perfect way to complete the day and to send the children away with positive feelings.

Circle sessions may be carried out wherever there is room for students to sit in a circle and experience few or no distractions. Most leaders prefer to have students sit in chairs rather than on the floor. Students seem to be less apt to invade one another's space while seated in chairs. Some leaders conduct sessions outdoors, with students seated in a secluded, grassy area.

How to Get Started

Teachers and counselors have used numerous methods to involve students in the circle process. What works well for one leader or class does not always work for another. Here are two basic strategies leaders have successfully used to get groups started. Whichever you use, we recommend that you post a chart listing the circle session rules and procedures to which every participant may refer.

1. Start one group at a time, and cycle through all groups. If possible, provide an opportunity for every student to experience a circle session in a setting where there are no disturbances. This may mean arranging for another staff member or aide to take charge of the students not participating in the circle. Non-participants may work on course work or silent reading, or, if you have a cooperative librarian, they may be sent to the library to work independently or in small groups on a class assignment. Repeat this procedure until all of the students have been involved in at least one circle session.

Next, initiate a class discussion about the circle sessions. Explain that from now on you will be meeting with each circle group in the classroom, with the remainder of the class present. Ask the students to help you plan established procedures for the remainder of the class to follow.

Meet with each circle session group on a different day, systematically cycling through the groups.

2. Combine inner and outer circles. Meet with one circle session group while another group listens and observes as an outer circle. Then have the two groups change places, with the students on the outside becoming the inner circle, and responding verbally to the topic. If you run out of time in middle-school classrooms, use two class periods for this. Later, a third group may be added to this alternating cycle. The end product of this arrangement is two or more groups (comprising everyone in the class) meeting together simultaneously. While one group is involved in discussion, the other groups listen and observe as members of an outer circle. Invite the members of the outer circle to participate in the review and discussion phases of the circle.

Managing the Rest of the Class

A number of arrangements can be made for students who are not participating in circle sessions. Here are some ideas:

• Arrange the room to ensure privacy. This may involve placing a circle of chairs or carpeting in a corner, away from other work areas. You might construct dividers from existing furniture, such as bookshelves or screens, or simply arrange chairs and tables in such a way that the circle area is protected from distractions.

• Involve aides, counselors, parents, or fellow teachers. Have an aide conduct a lesson with the rest of the class while you meet with a circle group. If you do not have an aide assigned to you, use auxiliary staff or parent volunteers.

• Have students work quietly on subject-area assignments in pairs or small, task-oriented groups.

• Utilize student aides or leaders. If the seat-work activity is in a content area, appoint students who show ability in that area as "consultants," and have them assist other students.

• Give the students plenty to do. List academic activities on the board. Make materials for quiet individual activities available so that students cannot run out of things to do and be tempted to consult you or disturb others.

• Make the activity of students outside the circle enjoyable. When you can involve the rest of the class in something meaningful to them, students will probably be less likely to interrupt the circle.

• Have the students work on an ongoing project. When they have a task in progress, students can simply resume where they left off, with little or no introduction from you. In these cases, appointing a "person in charge," "group leader," or "consultant" is wise.

• Allow individual journal-writing. While a circle is in progress, have the other students make entries in a private (or share-with-teacher-only) journal. The topic for journal writing could be the same topic that is being discussed in the Sharing Circle. Do not correct the journals but, if you read them, be sure to respond to the entries with your own written thoughts, where appropriate.

Leading the Sharing Circle

This section is a thorough guide for conducting Sharing Circles. It covers major points to keep in mind and answers questions which will arise as you begin using the program. Please remember that these guidelines are presented to assist you, not to restrict you. Follow them and trust your own leadership style at the same time.

Sharing Circle Procedures for the Leader

1. Setting up the circle (1-2 minutes)

2. Reviewing the ground rules (1-2 minutes) *

3. Introducing the topic (1-2 minutes)

4. Sharing by circle members (12-18 minutes)

5. Reviewing what is shared (3-5 minutes) **

6. Summary discussion (2-8 minutes)

7. Closing the circle (less than 1 minute)

*optional after the first few sessions

**optional

Introducing the topic (1-2 minutes)

State the topic in your own words. Elaborate and provide examples as each activity suggests. Add clarifying statements of your own that will help the students understand the topic. Answer questions about the topic, and emphasize that there are no "right" responses. Finally, restate the topic, opening the session to responses (theirs and yours). Sometimes taking your turn first helps the students understand the aim of the topic. At various points throughout the session, state the topic again.

Just prior to leading a circle session, contemplate the topic and think of at least one possible response that you can make during the sharing phase.

Setting up the circle (1-2 minutes)

As you sit down with the students in the circle, remember that you are not teaching a lesson. You are facilitating a group of people. Establish a positive atmosphere. In a relaxed manner, address each student by name, using eye contact and conveying warmth. An attitude of seriousness blended with enthusiasm will let the students know that the circle session is an important learning experience — an activity that can be interesting and meaningful.

Reviewing the ground rules (1-2 minutes).

At the beginning of the first session, and at appropriate intervals thereafter, go over the rules for the circle session. They are shown at the right.

From this point on, demonstrate to the students that you expect them to remember and abide by the ground rules. Convey that you think well of them and know they are fully capable of responsible behavior. Let them know that by coming to the session they are making a commitment to listen and show acceptance and respect for the other students and you.

Sharing Circle Rules

1. Bring yourself to the circle and nothing else.

2. Everyone gets a turn to share, including the leader.

3. You can skip your turn if you wish.

4. Listen to the person who is sharing.

5. The time is shared equally.

6. Stay in your own space.

7. There are no interruptions, probing, put-downs, or gossip.

Sharing by circle members (12-18 minutes)

The most important point to remember is this: The purpose of the circle session is to give students an opportunity to express themselves and be accepted for the experiences, thoughts, and feelings they share. Avoid taking the action away from the circle members. They are the stars!

Reviewing what is shared (optional 3-5 minutes)

Besides modeling effective listening (the very best way to teach it) and positively reinforcing students for attentive listening, a review can be used to deliberately improve listening skills in circle members.

Reviewing is a time for reflective listening, when circle members feed back what they heard each other say during the sharing phase of the circle. Besides encouraging effective listening, reviewing provides circle members with additional recognition. It validates their experience and conveys the idea, "you are important," a message we can all profit from hearing often.

To review, a circle member simply addresses someone who shared, and briefly paraphrases what the person said ("John, I heard you say....").

The first few times you conduct reviews, stress the importance of checking with the speaker to see if the review accurately summarized the main things that were shared. If the speaker says, "No," allow him or her to make corrections. Stress, too, the importance of speaking directly to the speaker, using the person's name and the pronoun "you," not "he" or "she." If someone says, "She said that...," intervene as promptly and respectfully as possible and say to the reviewer, "Talk to Betty...Say you." This is very important. The person whose turn is being reviewed will have a totally different feeling when talked *to*, instead of *about*.

Note: Remember that the review is optional and is most effective when used occasionally, not as a part of every circle.

Summary discussion (2-8 minutes)

The summary discussion is the cognitive portion of the circle session. During this phase, the leader asks thought-provoking questions to stimulate free discussion and higher-level thinking. Each circle session in this book includes summary questions; however, at times you may want to formulate questions that are more appropriate to the level of understanding in your group—or to what was actually shared in the circle. If you wish to make connections between the circle session topic and your content area, ask questions that will accomplish that objective and allow the summary discussion to extend longer.

It is important that you not confuse the summary with the review. The review is optional; the summary is not. The summary meets the need of people of all ages to find meaning in what they do. Thus, the summary serves as a necessary culmination to each circle session by allowing the students to clarify the key concepts they gained from the session.

Closing the circle (less than 1 minute).

The ideal time to end a circle session is when the summary discussion reaches natural closure. Sincerely thank everyone for being part of the circle. Don't thank specific students for speaking, as doing so might convey the impression that speaking is more appreciated than listening alone. Then close the circle by saying, "The circle session is over," or "OK, that ends our session."

More about Sharing Circle Procedures and Rules

The next few paragraphs offer further clarification concerning circle session leadership.

Why should students bring themselves to the circle and nothing else? Individual teachers differ on this point, but most prefer that students not bring objects (such as pencils, books, etc.) to the circle that may be distracting.

Who gets to talk? Everyone. The importance of acceptance in Sharing Circles cannot be overly stressed. In one way or another practically every ground rule says one thing: accept one another. When you model acceptance of students, they will learn how to be accepting. Each individual in the circle is important and deserves a turn to speak if he or she wishes to take it. Equal opportunity to become involved should be given to everyone in the circle.

Circle members should be reinforced equally for their contributions. There are many reasons why a leader may become more enthused over what one student shares than another. The response may be more on target, reflect more depth, be more entertaining, be philosophically more in keeping with one's own point of view, and so on. However, students need to be given equal recognition for their contributions, even if the contribution is to listen silently throughout the session.

In most of the circle sessions, plan to take a turn and address the topic, too. Students usually appreciate it very much and learn a great deal when their teachers and counselors are willing to tell about their own experiences, thoughts, and feelings. In this way you let your students know that you acknowledge your own humanness.

Does everyone have to take a turn? No. Students may choose to skip their turns. If the circle becomes a pressure situation in which the members are coerced in any way to speak, it will become an unsafe place where participants are not comfortable. Meaningful discussion is unlikely in such an atmosphere. By allowing students to make this choice, you are showing them that you accept their right to remain silent if that is what they choose to do.

As you begin circles, it will be to your advantage if one or more students decline to speak. If you are imperturbable and accepting when this happens, you let them know you are offering them an opportunity to experience something you think is valuable, or at least worth a try, and not attempting to force-feed them. You as a leader should not feel compelled to share a personal experience in every session, either. However, if you decline to speak in most of the sessions, this may have an inhibiting effect on the students' willingness to share.

A word should also be said about how this ground rule has sometimes been carried to extremes. Sometimes leaders have bent over backwards to let students know they don't have to take a turn. This seeming lack of enthusiasm on the part of the leader has caused reticence in the students. In order to avoid this outcome, don't project any personal insecurity as you lead the session. Be confident in your proven ability to work with students. Expect something to happen and it will.

Some circle leaders ask the participants to raise their hands when they wish to speak, while others simply allow free verbal sharing without soliciting the leader's permission first. Choose the procedure that works best for you, but do not call on anyone unless you can see signs of readiness.

Some leaders have reported that their first circles fell flat—that no one, or just one or two students, had anything to say. But they continued to have circles, and at a certain point everything changed. Thereafter, the students had a great deal to say that these leaders considered worth waiting for. It appears that in these cases the leaders' acceptance of the right to skip turns was a key factor. In time most students will contribute verbally when they have something they want to say, and when they are assured there is no pressure to do so.

Sometimes a silence occurs during a circle session. Don't feel you have to jump in every time someone stops talking. During silences students have an opportunity to think about what they would like to share or to contemplate an important idea they've heard. A general rule of thumb is to allow silence to the point that you observe group discomfort. At that point move on. Do not switch to another topic. To do so implies you will not be satisfied until the students speak. If you change to another topic, you are telling them you didn't really mean it when you said they didn't have to take a turn if they didn't want to.

If you are bothered about students who attend a number of circles and still do not share verbally, reevaluate what you consider to be involvement. Participation does not necessarily mean talking. Students who do not speak are listening and learning.

How can I encourage effective listening?

The Sharing Circle is a time (and place) for students and leaders to strengthen the habit of listening by doing it over and over again. No one was born knowing how to listen effectively to others. It is a skill like any other that gets better as it is practiced. In the immediacy of the circle session, the members become keenly aware of the necessity to listen, and most students respond by expecting it of one another.

In the Sharing Circle, listening is defined as the respectful focusing of attention on individual speakers. It includes eye contact with the speaker and open body posture. It eschews interruptions of any kind. When you conduct a circle session, listen and encourage listening in the students by (1) focusing your attention on the person who is speaking, (2) being receptive to what the speaker is saying (not mentally planning your next remark), and (3) recognizing the speaker when she finishes speaking, either verbally ("Thanks, Shirley") or nonverbally (a nod and a smile).

To encourage effective listening in the students, reinforce them by letting them know you have noticed they were listening to each other and you appreciate it. Occasionally conducting a review after the sharing phase also has the effect of sharpening listening skills.

How can I ensure the students get equal time?

When circle members share the time equally, they demonstrate their acceptance of the notion that everyone's contribution is of equal importance. It is not uncommon to have at least one dominator in a group. This person is usually totally unaware that by continuing to talk he or she is taking time from others who are less assertive.

Be very clear with the students about the purpose of this ground rule. Tell them at the outset how much time there is and whether or not you plan to conduct a review. When it is your turn, always limit your own contribution. If someone goes on and on, do intervene (dominators need to know what they are doing), but do so as gently and respectfully as you can.

What are some examples of put-downs?
Put-downs convey the message, "You are not okay as you are." Some put-downs are deliberate, but many are made unknowingly. Both kinds are undesirable in a Sharing Circle because they destroy the atmosphere of acceptance and disrupt the flow of discussion. Typical put-downs include:

* overquestioning.
* statements that have the effect of teaching or preaching
* advice giving
* one-upsmanship
* criticism, disapproval, or objections
* sarcasm
* statements or questions of disbelief

How can I deal with put-downs? There are two major ways for dealing with put-downs in circle sessions: preventing them from occurring and intervening when they do.

Going over the ground rules with the students at the beginning of each session, particularly in the earliest sessions, is a helpful preventive technique. Another is to reinforce the students when they adhere to the rule. Be sure to use nonpatronizing, nonevaluative language.

Unacceptable behavior should be stopped the moment it is recognized by the leader. When you become aware that a put-down is occurring, do whatever you ordinarily do to stop destructive behavior in the classroom. If one student gives another an unasked-for bit of advice, say for example, "Jane, please give Alicia a chance to tell her story." To a student who interrupts say, "Ed, it's Sally's turn." In most cases the fewer words, the better — students automatically tune out messages delivered as lectures.

Sometimes students disrupt the group by starting a private conversation with the person next to them. Touch the offender on the arm or shoulder while continuing to give eye contact to the student who is speaking. If you can't reach the offender, simply remind him or her of the rule about listening. If students persist in putting others down during circle sessions, ask to see them at another time and hold a brief one-to-one conference, urging them to follow the rules. Suggest that they reconsider their membership in the circle. Make it clear that if they don't intend to honor the ground rules, they are not to come to the circle.

How can I keep students from gossiping?
Periodically remind students that using names and sharing embarrassing information is not acceptable. Urge the students to relate personally to one another, but not to tell intimate details of their lives.

What should the leader do during the summary discussion? Conduct the summary as an open forum, giving students the opportunity to discuss a variety of ideas and accept those that make sense to them. Don't impose your opinions on the students, or allow the students to impose theirs on one another. Ask open-ended questions, encourage higher-level thinking, contribute your own ideas when appropriate, and act as a facilitator.

Bibliography and Resources

Armstrong, Thomas, *In Their Own Way: Discovering and Encouraging Your Child's Personal Learning Style*, Los Angeles: Jeremy P. Tarcher, Inc., 1987.

Arnold, William, W. and Plas, Jeanne M., *The Human Touch: Today's Most Unusual Program for Productivity and Profit*, New York: Wiley, 1993.

Berry, Diane. S. and Pennebaker, James W., "Nonverbal and Verbal Emotional Expression and Health," *Psychotherapy and Psychosomatics*, Vol 59, 1993.

Brody, Leslie R. and Hall, Judith A., "Gender and Emotion," *Handbook of Emotions*, New York: Guilford Press, 1993.

Caulfield, Joan and Jennings, Wayne, "Emotional Aspect of Brain Recognized," *Networker*, Winter 1996.

Cowan, David, *Taking Charge of Organizational Conflict*, Spring Valley, California: Innerchoice Publishing, 1995.

Davidson, Richard, *The Nature of Emotion: Fundamental Questions*, New York and Oxford: Oxford University Press, 1995.

Dreikers, Rudolf, *Psychodynamics and Counseling*, Chicago: Adler School of Professional Psychology, 1967.

Evans, Phil, *Motivation and Emotion*, London: Routledge, 1989.

Francis, Martha E. and Pennebaker, James W., "Talking and Writing as Illness Prevention." *Medicine, Exercise, Nutrition and Health*, American Journal of Health Promotion, Vol. 6, Issue 4, 1992.

Gardner, Howard, *Frames of Mind: The Theory of Multiple Intelligences*, New York: Basic Books, 1983.

Goleman, Daniel, *Emotional Literacy: A Field Report*, Fetzer Institute of Dalamazoo, Michigan, 1996.

Goleman, Daniel, "Emotional Intelligence: Why It Can Matter More Than IQ," *Learning*, May/June, 1996.

Goleman, Daniel, *Emotional Literacy: Why It Can Matter More Than IQ*, New York: Bantam, 1995.

Humphry, Nicholas, *A History of the Mind: Evolution and the Birth of Consciousness*, New York: Simon and Schuster, 1992.

Lazarus, Richard S., *Passion and Reason: Making Sense of Our Emotions*, New York and Oxford: Oxford Universaity Press, 1994.

Levenson, Robert W, "Human Emotion: A Functional View," *The Nature of Emotion: Fundamental Questions*, Oxford University Press, 1995.

Ralston, Faith, *Hidden Dynamics: How Emotions Affect Business Performance*, New York: American Management Association, 1995.

Richards, Dick, *Artful Work: Awakening Joy, Meaning, and Commitment in the Workplace*, San Francisco: Berrett-Koehler Publishers, 1995.

Saarni, Carolyn, "Emotional Competence: How Emotions and Relationships Become Integrated," in Thompson, R.A., *Socioemtional Development*, Lincoln and London: University of Nebraska Press, 1990.

Salovey, Peter, and Mayer, John D., "Emotional Intelligence," *Imagination, Cognition, and Personality 9*, 1990.

Solomon, Robert C., *The Passions: Emotions and the Meaning of Life*, Indianapolis and Cambridge: Hacket Publishing Company, 1993.

Vail, Priscilla, "The On Off Switch for Learning," *Connections: The Newletter of Social and Emotional Learning*, Collaborative for the Advancement of Social and Emotional Learning, Yale University, 1994.

Self-awareness

Activities in this unit teach students to:

- describe how personal changes brought about by growth and maturation are reflected in their feelings, values, and behavior.

- recognize how they have been affected by significant people in their lives.

- identify specific learnings, interests, abilities, strengths, weaknesses, accomplishments, feelings, and values.

Sharing Circles in this unit allow students to:

- describe a significant event in their lives and discuss how that event affected them emotionally.

- disclose something about themselves that is neither observable nor commonly known.

All the Me's I Am and Have Been
Dyad Sharing and Discussion

Objectives:

The students will:

—identify several different aspects of themselves.

—contrast desires and preferences experienced at different stages of growth.

—describe feelings associated with things that were/are important to them.

Materials:

chairs or other comfortable seating; stop watch

Procedure:

Ask the students to form dyads. Have the members of each dyad sit close, facing each other. Ask them to decide who will speak first. That person is A; and the other person is B.

Explain that you will be announcing topics for the students to talk about in their dyads. First A will talk to the topic while B listens for one minute. Then the process will reverse for another minute, with B talking and A listening.

When the class is ready, announce the following topics, making sure to time each minute accurately and signal the students to switch speakers or change topics.

Note: If your students are 12 or under, change age 10 (below) to age 8 and change age 12 (below) to 10.)

When I was five (years old), I felt...
When I was five, I liked to...
When I was 10, I liked to...
When I was 12, I really wanted...
Who I am now is...

Discussion Questions:

1. Did you and your partner share any similar experiences?
2. How do your experiences at younger ages affect you now?
3. How have your interests and desires changed over the years?
4. What else did you learn about yourself?

Significant People Who Have Affected My Life
Creative Writing and Discussion

Objectives:
The students will:
—describe one or more people who have been influential in their lives.
—discuss the impact of significant people on their beliefs and behaviors.

Materials:
none

Procedure:
Begin by discussing with the class how people can strongly affect other people's lives. Individuals whom we admire and respect become models. Through their bad examples, other people teach us how *not* to be.

Explain the writing assignment. Point out that the students will be writing about matters that are somewhat private. Ask them to think and write about one or more people who have significantly affected their lives, positively or negatively. Tell them to describe how each individual affected their beliefs, values, attitudes, habits, and/or goals. Add that in the cases of people who have had a negative influence, names and relationships should be omitted.

Allow the rest of the class period and about two-thirds of the next class period for writing.

Have the students form dyads, triads, or small groups and share their thoughts about the people who have significantly affected their lives. (Remind them to omit the names and relationships of those people who have affected them negatively.)

Discussion Questions:
1. How much of who you are seems to be influenced by other people?
2. If someone influences you, what part do you play in the changes that take place in you?
3. Can you think of a person who would say that you have been a significant person in his or her life?

Learning About Ourselves
Experience Sheet and Discussion

Objectives:
The students will:
—identify likes and dislikes and areas of strength and weakness.
—clarify personal values.
—explain how self-awareness facilitates performance.

Materials:
one copy of the experience sheet "Who Am I," for each student

Procedure:
Distribute the experience sheets and have the students answer the questions. When they have finished, facilitate a class discussion.

Discussion Questions:
1. What have you learned about your strengths and weaknesses from this activity?
2. What have you learned about you likes and dislikes?
3. What insights did you gain concerning your values?
4. How does knowing these kinds of things about yourself help you in school? ...in life?

Who Am I?
Experience Sheet

An important element of successful living is knowing who you are. In order to have life goals that are meaningful, realistic, and achievable, you need an accurate sense of self-understanding. You need to know your strengths and limitations, likes and dislikes, wants and needs, beliefs and values. The following questions will help you clarify these things.

Think back to some of the things you've learned to do in life. The following questions will get you started:

• What are some things you've learned quickly and easily? (List at least five. These do not have to be school subjects.)

1._____

2._____

3._____

4._____

5._____

• What is something that you learned because you kept working at it, even though it was hard?

_____

• What are some things you've been able to show other people how to do?

_____

• What are your major talents (strengths, abilities)?

_____

_____

• What are some of your major accomplishments?

_____

• In what school subject or activity are you most successful?

_____

What about weaknesses? First of all, everybody's got 'em. You aren't alone. Here are some things that other kids have trouble with. If any of these items apply to you, put a ✔ beside them.

___ 1. Using my time well
___ 2. Standing up for myself when I know I am right
___ 3. Overcoming shyness
___ 4. Building self-confidence
___ 5. Giving myself credit for achievements
___ 6. Giving myself credit for strengths
___ 7. Learning from my mistakes
___ 8. Acknowledging my present weaknesses
___ 9. Starting a conversation with a member of the opposite sex

Examine yourself closely, and complete as many of the following items as you can:

My personal strengths (talents, accomplishments, favorite activities, etc.):

1._____

2._____

3._____

4._____

5._____

My personal weaknesses (handicaps, difficulties, limitations, things I don't know how to do yet, etc.):

1._____

2._____

3._____

Now, complete the following half-sentences. Don't worry about being scrupulously honest or making perfect sense. Just have a good time looking at you.

I am a person who _____

_____

One thing I wish others could know about me is _____

_____

One of the things I feel proud of is _____

_____

It's hard for me to admit that _____

_____

One of the nicest things I could say about myself right now is _____

_____

A thing I accept in myself is _____

_____

A thing I can't accept in others is _____

_____

One thing that makes me angry is _____

_____

The best thing about being a child was_____

_____

The way I most need to improve is_____

_____

I am happy when _____

_____

I am sad when _____

_____

I am fearful when _____

_____

I feel lonely when _____

_____

I become frustrated when _____

_____

I hate it when _____

_____

I get excited when _____

_____

Admirable Qualities

List the ten qualities (such as honesty, bravery, helpfulness) you most admire in people.

1. _____   6. _____
2. _____   7. _____
3. _____   8. _____
4. _____   9. _____
5. _____   10. _____

How many of the qualities you listed do your friends have? How many do you have? What does that mean to you?

The next time you express an opinion, choose a movie or TV program, or buy something, stop and think about the values you are expressing.

A Significant Event in My Life
A Sharing Circle

Objectives:

The students will:
—identify important moments in their lives.
—describe the role their feelings play in determining the importance of an event.

Introduce the Topic:

Our topic is, "A Significant Event in My Life." There are many kinds of events that hold places of significance in our memories. What is one of the most significant that you can recall? It could be an achievement, such as winning an academic or athletic event or mastering a skill, or it could be a personal triumph, such as gaining control of a habit. Your significant event might be a move you made to new city or school. Or it might be a negative event, such as the death of a pet, or a divorce in the family. Think of one event in your life that you would like to share. Our topic is, "A Significant Event in My Life."

Discussion Questions:

1. How do you now whether an event in your life is significant or insignificant?
2. Who decides how much importance an event has?
3. How do you think you will feel in five or ten years about events that are significant to you now?

Something About Me You Wouldn't Know Unless I Told You
A Sharing Circle

Objectives:

The students will:

—share something about themselves that is neither obvious nor generally known.

—describe what it feels like to disclose information about themselves.

Introduce the Topic:

Today's topic is, "Something About me You Wouldn't Know Unless I Told You." No one can figure out everything about us just by observing us or being around us at school. For example, unless I told you, none of you would know about the great vacation I took over the summer, or the year I spent living in another country. There are many things in your life that we can't see or guess at either. So today, let's enlighten one another a bit. Let's share things about ourselves that no one else in the group knows.

Maybe you work as a volunteer at a hospital or for a group like the Red Cross. Maybe you help out with young children at your church or synagogue. Perhaps you like to write poetry, paint, square dance, clog, or weave baskets. Or you might have won a talent contest at some time. Think about it for a few moments and see of you can come up with something that will surprise us. The topic is, "Something About Me You Wouldn't Know Unless I Told You."

Discussion Questions:

1. How did it feel to talk about something that was kind of a "secret" until now?
2. Why do you suppose we don't learn these things about each other outside the Sharing Circle?
3. How can we avoid judging people based on the obvious and the superficial?

Additional Sharing Circle Topics

A Person I Admire
A Secret Wish I Have
Something I Like to Do Alone
The Craziest Dream I Ever Had
One Way I Wish I Could Be Different
Something I Want to Keep
Something I Like to Do with Others
When I Felt Comfortable Just Being Me
Something I Need Help With
My Favorite Place
My Idea of a Perfect Saturday Afternoon
Something About My Culture That I Appreciate
The Funniest Thing That Ever Happened to Me
My Favorite Vacation
Something I Like to Do With My Family
My Favorite Daydream
One of the Best Things That Ever Happened to Me
My Favorite Possession
Something I Really Like to Do
A Friend of Mine Who Is Different From Me
Something I Really Like to Do at School
If I Had One Wish It Would Be
One Way I Wish I Could Be Different
One Thing I Am Sure I Can Do Well
Something I Want
A Special Occasion or Holiday Related to My Culture
A Person I'd Like to Be Like

Managing Feelings

Activities in this unit teach students to:

- identify the thoughts that lead to feelings, and control feelings by modifying thought patterns.

- learn and practice a specific anger-management recipe.

- identify and express the feelings that precede and underlie anger, and recognize how much more productively others respond to "first feelings" than they do to expressions of anger.

Sharing Circles in this unit allow students to:

- describe incidents in which they handled their emotions well and discuss the mental processes that contributed to their success.

- describe secret fears, discuss the effects of being scared, and identify ways of mitigating fear.

I Think, Therefore I Feel
Experience Sheet and Discussion

Objectives:

The students will:

—describe the causal relationship between thoughts and feelings.

—state that their feelings in a situation can be improved by changing their thoughts about the situation.

—identify personal characteristics/traits that can and cannot be changed.

Materials:

one copy of the experience sheet, "You *Can* Help How You Feel!" for each student; chalkboard or chart paper

Procedure:

On chalkboard or chart paper, make three columns. Over the first column, write the heading, "Situation." Over the second, write the heading, "Thoughts" and over the third, write the heading, "Feelings."

Begin by asking the students to help you generate a list of situations that typically lead to negative feelings. Responses might include:

• not knowing the answer when the teacher calls on me
• doing poorly on a test for which I studied hard
• eating lunch alone
• not being invited to a friend's party
• being eliminated during tryouts for a team, musical group, cheer leading squad, school play, etc.
• when a boy/girl I like doesn't like me

List the situations in the first column. Then take one situation at a time and ask the students what <u>thoughts</u> a person might be likely to have in that situation. For example, a student who has to eat lunch alone might think, "I'm not fun (popular, attractive) enough." A student who doesn't know the answer to a teacher's question might think, "I always end up looking stupid." Write all suggestions in the second column.

Then ask the students how they would <u>feel</u> in each situation if they had the thoughts described. For example, a person eating alone who thinks she isn't popular might feel *humiliated* or *depressed*. The person who thinks he looks stupid because he can't answer a question might feel *embarrassed* or *frustrated*. Continue making connections between the thoughts and subsequent feelings in each situation.

Suggest to the students that the feelings in each situation can be improved by changing the thoughts from negative to neutral or positive. For example, what would happen to the feelings of the student who couldn't answer his teacher's question if he thought, "I don't know the answer, but I'll listen and find out what the answer is so I'll know it next time." Make the point that situations don't cause feelings, *thoughts* cause feelings. No one forces a person to feel a certain way in a particular situation. Suggest this idea: <u>The easiest way to change your feelings about a situation is to change your thoughts about it.</u>

Explain that using this technique can be especially helpful when dealing with physical characteristics that are out of one's control. For example, you might tell the students: *If it really bothers you that you are so tall, there's not much you can do to become shorter, but you could stop telling yourself that being tall is a curse and try focusing on your positive qualities instead.*

Distribute the experience sheets. Give the students a few minutes to write down their ideas under each example. Then have them form small groups, discuss their responses, and collectively generate additional ideas. Lead a follow-up discussion.

Discussion Questions:

1. How do thoughts trigger feelings?
2. Why is it easier to change your thoughts about a situation than it is to change your feelings?
3. Why do we waste our time feeling miserable about things that we cannot change?
4. Who is in control of your thoughts? ... of your feelings?

You Can Help How You Feel
Experience Sheet

You probably have things about yourself that you wish you could change. Some of those traits or characteristic can be changed—and some can't. But even if a trait cannot be changed, you don't have to feel miserable or depressed about it. Remember, negative feelings are caused by negative thoughts. The easiest way to stop feeling bad about a trait or characteristic is to change your thoughts about it.

So, instead of feeling embarrassed, self-conscious, or depressed about a trait, choose to do one of two things:
1. Change (or minimize) the trait.
2. Change your thoughts about the trait.

What could you do in each of these situations. Write down your ideas:

1. You dislike the color of your hair and think it makes you look drab.

_____

_____

2. You are very short, and think that short people have to fight for attention and respect.

_____

_____

3. Your friend says brown hair is boring. You have brown hair, and think he or she is just trying to make you feel bad. Now you hate your hair.

_____

_____

4. You are self-conscious about your weight (too fat or too thin).

_____

_____

5. You think you are awkward and uncoordinated._____

_____

_____

_____

6. You hate your nose._____

_____

_____

7. You use a wheelchair and think everyone feels sorry for you, which causes you to feel resentful.

_____

_____

8. You think your feet are too big._____

_____

_____

9. You have a speech impediment and think it's not worth it to try to communicate with people.

_____

_____

10. You are self-conscious about your freckles. _____

_____

_____

11. You are shy. You'd like to make friends more easily, but have trouble starting conversations and getting to know other kids.

_____

_____

_____

Taking Charge of Personal Anger
Dyad and Large Group Discussion

Objectives:
The students will:
—describe how they typically react when they are angry.
—examine a simple process for managing anger.
—discuss the importance of "buying time" when they are angry.

Materials:
chalkboard and chalk

Procedure:
Prior to class, write the following Anger Management Recipe on the board:

Anger Management Recipe
1. Buy yourself some time!
2. Ask yourself these questions:
—*Is this situation in any way similar to an experience from my past?*
—*How important is my relationship with this person?*
—*What other things are going on in my life right now?*
—*What's at risk in this situation?*

Introduce the activity by asking the students: *How many of you have heard that the best thing to do when you are angry is to count to ten? Where do you suppose that idea came from?*

Facilitate student input, jotting ideas on the board. Briefly elaborate at appropriate points, referring to the "Anger Management Recipe" on the board and incorporating the following ideas:

- Counting to ten allows time to calm down and gain control.
- We may be reacting to the situation because it reminds us of one from our past that didn't go well. It's like a reflex — probably a defensive one.
- Something that happened in the past may cause us to overreact emotionally or feel like the problem is more important than it really is.
- If our relationship with the other person is important, we're more likely to put time and effort into resolving the conflict.
- The more we value the relationship or the issue that is causing our anger, the more we have to lose if the conflict doesn't go well.
- Anger is the by-product of almost every conflict.
- Conflict situations arise, and as we think about what's going on, we get angry.
- As we become angry, our bodies are charged with chemicals that give us negative feelings. By buying some time (it actually takes longer than just counting to ten; it takes about 20 minutes) we allow these chemicals to dissipate and our feelings of anger begin to go away.
- Our anger can infect others, making them angry.
- Since our anger is caused by our thoughts, we can reduce anger by changing the thoughts that precede it.
- When anger goes unmanaged, it can add fuel to a conflict and cause it to escalate. As one negative thought leads to another, anger increases and the conflict grows in size.

Have the students form pairs. Tell them to take 2 minutes each to describe the very first thing they typically do when they feel angry. (Signal the students when it is time to change speakers.)

After each student has shared, reconvene the group and ask the students to call out the behaviors they described to their partners while you list them on the board. When you have finished, point to the list and ask:

— *When you respond this way, do you think about it first, or is your reaction automatic?*

—*If it's automatic (a style of responding), how can you make your first response more reasoned (a strategy for responding)?*

Clarify that time is what is usually needed in order to choose an effective strategy instead of simply reacting. Go back to the recipe on the board and review the steps. Facilitate a culminating discussion.

Discussion Questions:

1. In what ways can the Anger Management Recipe help you?
2. What is the hardest thing about following this recipe?
3. Why is it difficult to stay in control when you are angry?
4. What is the most important ingredient in the recipe? Explain.

Extension:

Have the students participate in a second dyad in which they describe to their partner what they typically do when anger is directed at them.

First Feelings
Experience Sheet and Discussion

Objectives:

The students will:

—learn and practice acceptable ways to express negative emotions.

—identify feelings that typically precede/precipitate anger and identify ways to deal with them.

Materials:

one copy of the experience sheet, "Getting a Handle on Hostility," for each student

Procedure:

Write the heading, "Anger" on the chalkboard. Ask the class to brainstorm specific examples of angry behavior. List them beneath the heading. Then ask the students to describe how their bodies feel when they are angry, and talk briefly about the power of the emotion.

Read the following scenario to the class:

Desiree skipped out of her classroom happily. On her way home she boasted to her friend, Antonio, "All I have to do for homework is math, and it's a cinch. Math is my easiest subject. I always get A's." She ran into her house and threw down her backpack. Off she rushed to play with friends until dinner. That evening she played games with her sister and watched some television, forgetting to do her homework. The next day in school, when her teacher asked for her Math homework, Desiree looked startled and then turned red. "I forgot to do it," she said, looking down at her backpack. As she looked up, Antonio was watching her from across the room. Desiree suddenly stuck her tongue out at him and wouldn't look at him for the rest of the morning. At recess she refused to play ball with Antonio and told him she was mad at him.

Following the story, facilitate discussion by asking these questions:

1. What were Desiree's *first feelings* when she realized that she had forgotten her homework?
2. How could she have expressed those feelings?
3. How did Desiree feel when she saw her friend Antonio watching her?
4. Why did she refuse to play with Antonio at recess?
5. How could Desiree have expressed her feelings toward Antonio?
6. What could she have done to control her behavior toward her friend?

Make the following points in a discussion about anger:

• Anger is a normal emotion. We all get angry and need to learn acceptable and effective ways to deal with anger.
• Anger tends to be a <u>secondary</u> feeling or emotion. In other words, one or more *other* feelings usually precede anger. For example, when Desiree realized she had forgotten to do her homework, her first emotions may have been shock, humiliation, panic, regret, and desperation in rapid succession.

- Another example: When a student fails a test for which she or he studied hard, the first feelings are overwhelming disappointment and frustration. But anger follows so quickly that it's the only emotion the rest of the class observes. The same thing happens with other feelings, too.
- Other people usually have difficulty coping with someone's anger. This is partly because anger acts as a mask, hiding what is really going on. Others will have a much easier time responding to your frustration, grief, relief, sadness, or fear than to your anger. Consequently, a very valuable skill to develop is the skill of expressing your initial feelings, rather than just your anger.
- Anger puts stress on the body. Too much anger experienced too often can lead to illness.

Distribute the experience sheet, "Dealing with Anger." Go over the directions and give the students a few minutes to respond to the questions individually.

Have the students form small groups. Ask them to discuss the situations and their responses to the questions.

Discussion Questions:

1. What did you decide were Marco's first emotions? Jed's? Nieko's?
2. How could each character have expressed his or her first emotions?
3. What other behaviors did you come up with in each situation?
4. How does anger mask what is really going on?
5. Why is anger such a difficult emotion to deal with in other people?
6. If you have difficulty dealing with anger, what can you do to get help?

Extension:

Have volunteers role play several of the best alternatives suggested in each situation.

Dealing with Anger
Experience Sheet

Situation 1:

Marco and Jed were best buddies. After school, they often stayed on the playground to play their favorite game, tether ball. During one game, as they were batting the ball back and forth with their hands, Marco suddenly spotted his dog running loose across the playground. "Here, Rambo," he shouted, as Jed slammed the ball his way. Marco felt the impact of the rapidly flying ball right on the side of his face, and fell to the ground. After rubbing his stinging face and catching his breath, Marco got up and started screaming at Jed. "Hey, you did that on purpose, you jerk." With tears streaming down his face, he ran toward his friend swinging his fists and shouting, "I am gonna get you back!" Backing away, Jed yelled, "It's your own fault, dummy. You weren't watching the ball!"

Questions:

What were Marco's first feelings after he fell to the ground?

_____

How did he express those feelings?_____

_____

How did Jed react to Marco's actions? _____

_____

How could Marco have better expressed his first feelings?

_____

_____

How would Jed have reacted if Marco had expressed his first feelings well?

_____

_____

Situation 2:

Mieko had been attending gymnastics class in the evenings at the local gymnasium. She liked to do tumbling and easily performed handsprings, cartwheels, and flips. However, when it was her turn to work on the balance beam, Mieko didn't do all of the movements easily. One evening, Mieko was practicing turns on the beam and kept falling off. She just couldn't keep her balance. After practice, when Mieko's coach asked her to stay for a few minutes so he could give her some tips on how to keep her balance, she picked up her things and stormed out of the gym, slamming the door behind her. "He's just picking on me," Mieko grumbled as she stomped down the street.

Questions:

How do you think Mieko felt when she kept falling off the balance beam?

_____

What were Mieko's <u>first</u> feelings when the coach asked her to stay after practice?

_____

How did she express those feelings?

_____

What could Mieko have said or done to effectively express her <u>first</u> feelings?

_____

_____

How do you think the coach reacted when Mieko walked out?

_____

How would the coach have reacted to Mieko's <u>first</u> feelings? Would he have understood how she felt?

_____

_____

A Time I Handled My Feelings Well
A Sharing circle

Objectives:
The students will:
—identify ways to express and deal with feelings.
—demonstrate a positive attitude about self.

Introduce the topic.
We all face situations that cause us to experience strong feelings. How we behave at those times depends on how well we take charge of our feelings. Today, we're going to talk about instances when the outcome was good. Our topic is, "A Time I Handled My Feelings Well."

For example, maybe you wanted a special gift for your birthday or Christmas and didn't receive it because your parents either failed to realize how important it was to you or couldn't afford it. Since you didn't want to hurt their feelings, you didn't express your disappointment to them, but told a friend instead. Perhaps you were very angry at someone and wanted to hit the person, but instead managed to talk to him or her and express your angry feelings without hitting. Maybe You lost a game or an election and really wanted to yell, but instead congratulated the winner. Possibly you injured yourself and it hurt so badly that you needed to cry, so you did. Handling your feelings well usually means doing what is appropriate, without hurting someone else in the process. Think of a situation that you feel okay sharing. When you are ready, raise your hand. The topic is, "A Time I Handled My Feelings Well."

Discussion Questions:
1. What similarities were there in the ways we handled our feelings? What differences were there?
2. If our feelings are always acceptable, why isn't our behavior always acceptable?
3. What do we have to control, our feelings or our behavior? How can we do that?

A Secret Fear I Have
A Sharing Circle

Objectives:

The students will:

—describe fears that they usually keep to themselves.

—discuss ways in which fears can be managed.

Introduce the Topic:

The topic of today's Sharing Circle is, "A Secret Fear I Have." A secret is something no one else knows about. Fear is an emotion that causes us distress, anxiety, or a sense of dread. All of us probably harbor secrets about ourselves, things we don't want anyone else to know. Perhaps we keep such things to ourselves because we think people won't like or accept us if they know; we are afraid they might laugh or make fun of us. Just as we all have secrets, we also have fears. Everyone is afraid of something. You may fear the dark, lightening and thunder, or strange dogs. You may have a fear of flying or being in high places. You may fear getting lost, being alone, swimming in deep water, or some other situation or thing. Think for a moment about a secret fear you have and are willing to share with us. Our topic is, "A Secret Fear I Have."

Discussion Questions:

1. What is something that we all have in common, based on what we shared?
2. How did it feel to share a secret? How do you feel now after taking that risk?
3. What have you learned about yourself from thinking or sharing on this topic?
4. What steps can we take to overcome our fears, or handle them better?

Additional Sharing Circle Topics

A Time I Felt Happy

A Feeling of Sadness I Remember

A Time I Felt Scared

A Time I Felt Unhappy

How I React When I'm Angry

A Time I Couldn't Control My Curiosity

A Time I Got My Feelings Hurt

A Favorite Feeling

Someone Who Respects My Feelings

A Time I Felt Excited

I Felt Good and Bad About the Same Thing

Something I Hate to Do

How Somebody Hurt My Feelings

How I Feel When People Tell Me They Like Me

Something in My Life That I'm Happy About

I Could Have Hurt Someone's Feelings, But Didn't

A Feeling I Had a Hard Time Accepting

A Time I Was Alone But Not Lonely

A Thought I Have That Makes Me Feel Happy

A Time When It Was Okay to Express My Feelings

I Told Someone How I Was Feeling

I Did Something Impulsive and Regretted It Later

A Time I Really Controlled My Feelings

A Time I Was Afraid to Do Something But Did It Anyway

A Time I Helped Someone Who Was Afraid

A Time I was Scared and It Was Fun

A Way I Get Over Being Afraid

Decision Making

Activities in this unit teach students to:

- use a six-step decision-making process.

- examine factors that affect decisions, including alternatives, facts and information, and values.

- recognize the consequences of procrastination, particularly when important decisions need to be made.

Sharing Circles in this unit allow students to:

- explore feeling and thought processes involved in making difficult decisions.

- describe what it is like to make a decision that is well researched and based on facts as opposed to impulse or emotion.

Making a Good Decision
Experience Sheet and Discussion

Objectives:
The students will:

—learn and practice a basic decision-making process.

—describe the importance of alternatives in decision making.

—explain how values, goals, and personal preferences affect decisions.

Materials:
pencil and one copy of the experience sheet, "Decisions, Decisions!" for each student

Procedure:
Distribute the experience sheets. Read through the decision-making steps with the students, clarifying each one. Here are some ideas to discuss and questions to ask:

• Knowing what is important to you and what you want to accomplish involves such things as likes/dislikes, values, and interests. Most important, it involves having goals.

• You can get information by talking to people, visiting places, watching T.V., and reading. Once you have the information, you must be able to evaluate it. If two people tell you to do opposite things, how are you going to know which is right? What if neither is right?

• Look into the future. Ask yourself what would happen if you chose each of the alternatives available. For example, what would happen if:

—you did not go to college?

—you never got married?

—you ran away from home?

—you dropped out of school?

—you became a professional rock singer?

How did you make your predictions? What information did you use?

• When you reach the decision point, don't freeze up. If you've done a good job on the other steps, you can choose the best alternative with confidence. Remember, if you *don't* choose, someone else may choose for you.

• Not every decision requires an action plan, but the big ones usually do. The decision to visit your grandparents in another state next summer won't come true unless you make it. And that means more decisions. Can you think what they are?

Give the students time to complete the experience sheet. As they work, circulate and offer assistance. (To allow more time, let the students complete the experience sheet as homework.)

Have the students choose partners. Ask them to take turns sharing their decision and decision-making process. Lead a follow-up discussion.

Discussion Questions

1. What did you learn about decision-making from this activity?
2. What can happen if you put off making a decision?
3. Why is it important to know your interests and values when making decisions?
4. How can having goals help you make decisions?
5. Why is it helpful to have several alternatives to choose from?
6. If you don't have alternatives, how can you develop them?

Decisions, Decisions
Experience Sheet

The decision-making process involves <u>using what you know (or can learn) to get what you want.</u> Here are some steps to follow when you have a decision to make:

1. **Define the decision to be made.**
2. **Know what is important to you and what you want to accomplish.**
3. **Study the information you already have. Get and study new information, too.**
4. **Look at each alternative and ask yourself what will happen to you and the other people involved if you choose it.**
5. **Make a decision.**
6. **Develop a plan for putting your decision into action.**

Think of a decision that you need to make. Write a description of it here:

a_____

a_____

a_____

Now follow steps 2 through 6. Use these lines for your notes:

a_____

a_____

a_____

a_____

a_____

a_____

a_____

a_____

Factoring a Decision
Writing and Discussion

Objectives:
The students will:
—define the term *decision making*.
—describe and analyze a recent decision.
—discuss factors that affect decision-making

Materials:
chalkboard and chalk; writing materials for the students

Procedure:
Write the following statements on the chalkboard for the students to see when they enter the classroom. (If you prefer, prepare and distribute a handout of the statements.)

1. A decision is not necessary unless there is more than one alternative to choose from.
2. Not deciding is making a decision.
3. Learning decision-making skills increases the possibility that I can have what I want.
4. Each decision is limited by what I am *able* to do. For example, if I cannot ride a bike, I cannot choose between biking and walking.
5. The more alternatives I know about, the more I am *able* to do.
6. Each decision is also limited by what I am *willing* to do.
7. What I am willing to do is usually determined by what I *value* (believe in) most.

Introduce the activity. Ask the students to help you define the term *decision making*. Record their suggestions on the chalkboard and discuss. Through consensus, try to arrive at a simple definition that focuses on the aspect of choice, such as:

Decision-making is when a person selects from two or more possible choices.

Ask the students to look at the prepared list of statements. Briefly read through and discuss the statements. Then assign each student one statement. (Number the students off from one to seven and tell them to match their number to a statement.)

Explain the writing assignment. Tell the students that you want them to write about a decision they faced recently and how it relates to their statement. Say to them: *Think of a decision. It can be a big decision like whether or not to go to summer camp, or a very small one like what to eat for breakfast. Describe the decision. Then explain how your statement about decision-making relates to that decision. For example, if your decision is whether or not to go to summer camp, and your decision-making statement is, "The more alternatives I know about, the more I am able to do, " you might explain that if you hadn't known a camp was available, you wouldn't have been able to make that decision. Or, because you knew about two different camps, a summer junior astronaut program, and a backyard swim program, you were (potentially) able to do more than if you had known about only one camp.*

When the students have finished their papers, have them form small groups. Tell the 1's to get together, the 2's to get together, etc. Ask them to take turns sharing what they wrote with the group. Encourage them to discuss each person's writing in relation to the group's decision-making statement and any other statements from the list that they think apply. If you like, have the students edit each other's papers. (Rewriting can be assigned as homework.)

Discussion Questions:

1. Were there any decisions for which the decision-making statements were not true?
2. What did you learn about decision-making from this activity?
3. How do your beliefs affect decision-making? Your attitudes? Your feelings? Your likes and dislikes? Your previous experiences?
4. What can you do to increase your alternatives in a decision-making situation? (research of various kinds)

If I Ignore It, It Might Go Away
Creative Dramatics and Discussion

Objectives:
The students will:
—demonstrate the dynamics of procrastination.
—discuss problems associated with postponing decisions.

Procedure:
Introduce the activity. Explain to the students that you would like three to five volunteers to participate in creating, rehearsing, and performing a short, 2- to 5-minute skit.

Explain the assignment to the volunteers. Tell them that you would like them to demonstrate the meaning of, "If I Ignore It, It Might Go Away," by creating a dramatic situation in which someone refuses to make a decision about something that requires immediate action. In addition to the decision-maker, the actors may play the parts of victims, persecutors, would-be rescuers, and other characters, such as advisors, distracters, and pressurers.

Designate a quiet, private place where the actors can create and practice their skit. Give them at least 20 minutes to prepare for their performance before the class. After the skit has been performed, conduct a class discussion.

Discussion Questions:
1. What did you learn about decision-making from this skit?
2. How did you feel toward (the character who ignored the necessity to make a decision)?
3. What can happen when we put off making decisions for too long?
4. How do you feel about yourself when you put off making a necessary decision?
5. What can you do to ensure that you make decisions in a timely way?
6. How did you make decisions when you were creating your skits?
7. What problems did you encounter?
3. What might you do differently in your next group decision-making task?

I Had a Hard Time Choosing Between Two Things
A Sharing Circle

Objectives:
The students will:
—identify choices they have made.
—explain that choosing one thing often means giving up others.

Introduce the Topic:
Our topic for this session has to do with decision making, and I'm sure all of us will be able to relate to it. Have you ever been in a situation where you were torn between two things and couldn't make up your mind? If so, you'll appreciate this topic. It is, "I Had a Hard Time Choosing Between Two Things."

Tell us about a time when you had to choose one thing over another because we couldn't have both. Maybe you wanted to go to two different places at the same time, or you wanted to buy two things and only had enough money for one. Or describe some other type of situation in which you had to choose between two different things. Think about it for a few moments. The topic is, "I Had a Hard Time Choosing Between Two Things."

Discussion Questions:
1. How did you feel about giving up the thing you didn't choose?
2. How is making a decision the same thing as taking a risk?
3. Someone once said that after you make your decision, you need to move out of "what if " and move into "it is, " What does that mean?
4. Is the best choice for one person the best choice for everyone? Why?

I Made a Decision Based on the Facts
A Sharing Circle

Objectives:

The students will:

—recognize the importance of making fair decisions

—describe how weighing facts and evidence contributes to making fair decisions.

Introduce the Topic:

Our topic for this session is, "I Made a Decision Based on the Facts." Have you ever been in a situation where you had to decide something, and you wanted to be very fair? If you have, then you probably realize that to be fair you have to set aside your own feelings and try to look at facts and information. For instance, maybe you were asked to help choose a new team member for soccer or Little League. You couldn't simply choose the person you liked best; you had to choose the best player. Perhaps you had to decide the winner in some kind of contest. Instead of giving the prize to your best friend, you awarded it to the person who did the best job. Or maybe you had to help settle an argument between two younger children. To make a fair decision, you needed to hear both sides and gather as much information as you could. We all have many opportunities to make fair decisions. Tell us about one that you made. Take a few moments to think about it. The topic is, "I Made a Decision Based on the Facts."

Discussion Questions:

1. How did you feel when you were making a decision in the situation you shared?
2. What makes a decision fair?
3. Why do people make decisions without looking at the facts?
4. If you have to make a decision and don't have enough information, what can you do?

Additional Sharing Circle Topics

A Time I Had to Choose the Best of Two Bad Things
I Had a Problem and Solved It
I Didn't Want to Have to Make a Decision
I Thought Over My Decision, and I Stuck to It
A Time I Shared in Making a Decision
A Time I Used Good Judgment
I Thought It Over and Then Decided
Looking Back on a Decision I Made
A Time I Had Trouble Deciding the Right Thing to Do
I Had to Remake My Decision
What I Would Do If I Were an Adult
Something I Would Like to Achieve in the Next Three Years
Things I Can Do to Get Where I Want to Be
How I Earned Something and What I Did with It
I Put Off Making a Decision
A Decision I Lived to Regret
A Decision Someone Else Made That Affected Me
It Was My Decision, But Someone Else Made It
The Hardest Decision I've Ever Made
One of the Best Decisions I've Ever Made
I Made a Good Decision But Got a Poor Result
The Hardest Thing About Making Decisions Is...
The Easiest Thing About Making Decisions Is...
What It Takes to Be Decisive
A Time I Was Sure I Was Doing the Right Thing
I Time I Decided Based on My Feelings
A Time Someone Made an Unfair Decision
I Made a Decision and Regretted It Later

Managing Stress

Activities in this unit teach students to:

- practice three different meditation exercises to relieve stress.

- apply a formula that explains how stress is produced, and distinguish between stressors which they can and cannot control.

- use simple physical exercises to relieve stress.

Sharing Circles in this unit allow students to:

- identify situations that cause them stress and discuss coping behaviors.

- describe specific things they do to take care of their bodies and emotions.

Centering and Balancing
A Trio of Meditations

Objectives:

The students will:

—identify and label stressful situations associated with strong negative emotions

—practice simple meditation exercises that can be used to relieve stress and regain emotional "balance."

Materials:

For the music meditation, a cassette or CD player and a tape or disk of classical or "new age" relaxation music

Procedure:

Begin this activity by talking with the students about what it means to be *out of balance*. Start with bodily examples, which the students will relate to immediately, then move the discussion toward emotions. For example, ask: *How many of you have ever lost your balance?*

Ask two or three volunteers to demonstrate what happened when they lost their balance. Establish the concept of a center around which weight is distributed evenly when we are in balance, and that getting off balance usually means that too much weight has shifted to one side or another.

Then, in your own words, explain: *Losing our balance in gymnastics, walking along a wall, riding a bike, or skating are examples that occur on the outside, with our bodies. But we can get out of balance inside, too. One way we can get out of balance inside is from strong negative emotions. If we get very*

nervous or angry or afraid, we start to feel and act "out of control" or "unbalanced." Can you think of a time when you were out of balance because of negative feelings?

Invite several students to share experiences in which they felt controlled by negative emotions. List the emotions they mention on the board. Then explain further:

To get back in balance, we have to become centered again. Being centered inside means being quiet, calm, relaxed, and alert. Today, we're going to practice some simple exercises that will help us become centered.

Lead the students in one or more of the exercises on the following pages. When you have finished, facilitate a summary discussion, using the questions, page 68. Encourage the students to practice centering exercises whenever they feel stressed or out of balance.

Simple Meditation

Tell the students to sit comfortably and close their eyes. Then, slowly read this centering exercise in a soothing tone:

Take several deep breaths . . . Feel your body begin to relax. . . Breathe in and hold it . . . breathe out. . . Breathe in and hold it . . . breathe out. . . Focus your attention on your feet. . . Breathe in so deeply that you can feel the air move through your body . . . all the way to your toes.   . . Do that again . . . this time feel the air sweeping all the tension and negative feelings with it . . . Breathe out . . . releasing the tension . . . pushing out the negative feelings. . . Feel your body relax more and more with each breath. . . Feel your stomach relax . . . your heart . . . your chest . . . your shoulders . . . Keep breathing . . . deeply . . . until all of the tension has left your body. . . Then, when you are ready, bring your awareness back to this room and open your eyes.

Visual Meditation

Ask the students to pick out an object somewhere in the room and go sit near it. (It's okay if several students pick the same object, just as long as they can all gather around it without crowding one another. Explain that the object can be a book, ball, picture, flower, light fixture, etc. When all of the students have picked an object and are settled, say to them:

Focus all of your attention on the object. . . Fix your eyes on it . . . Without looking away, begin to breathe deeply and slowly. . . slowly and deeply. . . Let your body relax. . . Let your arms relax . . . let your shoulders relax . . . let your legs and feet relax . . . As you look at this object, begin to feel its energy . . . the energy that gives it shape . . . and color . . . the energy that attracted you to it . . . Let yourself connect with the energy in this object . . . Let any tension or negative feelings that you have flow out of you . . . and into this object . . . Keep breathing deeply . . . while you watch the tension leave you . . . and flow in a stream . . . across space . . . and into the object . . . Send all of it there . . . and relax . . . relax . . . relax. . . . . When you are completely relaxed, look away from the object and come back to this room.

Music Meditation

Accompany this meditation with a cassette or CD of relaxing classical or "new age" music. Tell the students to sit comfortably and close their eyes. Begin playing the music at a low volume while you give these directions:

Take several deep breaths. . . and, as you listen to the music. . . begin to relax your body . . . Relax your feet and legs . . . Relax your stomach and back . . . relax your chest . . . relax your arms and shoulders . . . relax your neck . . . and relax all the features of your face . . . . Now, breathe deeply . . . and imagine that you are breathing in the music . . . breathing it into your lungs . . . where it enters your blood . . . carried by millions of molecules of oxygen . . . to all parts of your body . . . Feel the music as it flows through your arms . . . and hands . . . to the tips of your fingers . . . Feel it flow through your heart . . . your stomach . . . into your legs . . . and your feet . . . all the way to your toes . . . Let the music wash away any last bit of tension left in your body . . . Feel it swirl over and around any negative feelings . . . and carry them away . . . Negative feelings have no power against this music . . . They simply disappear. . . . . so let them go . . . . and when they are all gone . . . open your eyes . . . and come back to this room.

Discussion Questions:

1. How did you feel when you were doing these relaxation exercises? How did you feel immediately afterwards?
2. Why is it important to stay in balance, or get back in balance when you are stressed?
3. When you feel stressed or upset, what happens to your ability to study and learn?
4. How might you use exercises like this on your own, at school or at home?

From Panic to Power
Class Discussion

Objectives:

The students will:

—describe causes of personal stress.

—explain how stress works.

—state that taking action to solve problems can relieve stress.

Materials:

easel; chart paper and marking pen or chalkboard and chalk

Procedure:

Tell the students that the group is going to spend some time talking about stress — what it is and what can be done about it. Begin by asking the students to name some things that cause them stress. Brainstorm with the students to achieve as long a list as possible.

Explain: *Here's a formula that explains stress.*

STRESSOR + PHYSICAL REACTION - ACTION = STRESS.

When we think we're in danger (of failing, being embarrassed, not getting what we want, etc.), our bodies react just like they would if we were in danger of being attacked by a lion. Adrenaline and hormones start pumping, our hearts beat faster, our muscles tense, and we get set for 'fight or flight.' Then if we don't take action — if we just sit around and worry, for example — all those unused hormones and tense muscles end up hurting us.

Next, go through the list, one item at a time, and have the students brainstorm actions they could take in each type of situation. For example, if they don't understand the current chapter in math, they can talk to the teacher, ask a parent for help, study with a friend, etc.

Empower the students by demonstrating enthusiasm about all the things they can do.

When the stressor is something the students have no control over (like the death of a pet) or little control over (like noisy neighbors), acknowledge that even though they can't "act on" the stressor directly, they can use stress reducers. Brainstorm and list a variety of stress management strategies.

Extension:

Act out some of the stressful situations. Concentrate on those over which the students have some control. Encourage the students to take turns dramatizing the different courses of action they could take. Lead a discussion after each dramatization.

Stress Breaks
A Movement Activity

Objective:
The students will:
—demonstrate specific techniques for relieving stress.
—describe the benefits of using exercise to relieve stress.

Materials:
large circle of chairs — one chair for each student

Procedure:
Ask the students to sit in a circle. Announce that the group is going to invent and practice "stress breaks" that can be used to reduce stress almost any time it occurs.

Explain: *One of best things you can do to relieve stress is exercise. And that doesn't just mean running a mile or playing a basketball game — almost any kind of stretching or moving can help get the tension out of muscles and make the heart beat faster. Think of a movement that you can do sitting down. You can pump your arm up and down, roll your shoulders backwards and forwards, or "run" very fast with your feet.* (Demonstrate several sitting exercises for the students.)

We're going to go around the circle and each one of you is going to lead us in a movement for 10 seconds. When it's your turn, show us a movement that no one else has done and we'll all do it with you.

Get the game started and keep it going at a lively pace. Participate along with the students.

After every student has led a movement, tell the students to stand and move their chairs out of the way. Go around the circle again, this time creating movements that can be done from a standing position. Demonstrate a few, like running in place, stretching to the side, etc.

Finally, have each student lead a "traveling" movement for 5-10 seconds. Maintain the circle formation. Suggest that skipping, hopping, jogging, etc., can be done using different kinds of arm movements for variation.

Note: This activity will generate much laughter and enjoyment. Welcome it, and point out that laughter relieves stress, too.

Discussion Questions:
1. When can you use stress breaks outside of class?
2. What is the value of exercise in relieving stress?
3. How does stress affect your ability to do schoolwork? ...homework?

Extension:
If you have ample space or can go outdoors, do the traveling part of the game in a snake formation, with the leader weaving about and the other students following. Include short "stress breaks" occasionally during class. Have the students take turns leading them.

A Time I Felt a Lot of Tension and Stress
A Sharing Circle

Objectives:

The students will:
—describe the effects of tension and stress on the body.

Introduce the Topic:

Our circle session topic for today is, "A Time I Felt a Lot of Tension and Stress." This is another of those very universal things that all people have probably felt at one time or another in their lives. When we become tense, our bodies react in a number of ways, usually by tightening muscles. Sometimes our stomach, vision, and hearing are affected. Other times we get headaches. When we become tense, sometimes we know it, and sometimes we don't.

Have you ever discovered that some part of you ached, like your stomach, neck, shoulders, back, or legs, and then realized that an hour or two earlier you were very upset about something? Perhaps you didn't realize just how upset you were when it was happening. Often tension and stress accompany unpleasant circumstances, but not always. For example, when you ride a galloping horse or a roller coaster, your body will undoubtedly be tense and your feelings may be very positive at the same time. The experience can be thrilling and exciting. See if you can remember a time when you experienced tension and stress, and if you will, tell us about it. The topic is, "A Time I Felt a Lot of Tension and Stress."

Discussion Questions:

1. When did you become aware of your tension?
2. What happens to your ability to think straight when you are stressed out?
3. What similarities did you notice in how we were affected by tension and stress?
4. Can you think of ways you can care for yourself after (maybe even during) a tense situation?

Something I Do for My Own Well-Being
A Sharing Circle

Objectives:

The students will:
—describe a way they manage stress.
—discuss the importance of taking responsibility for their own well-being.

Introduce the Topic:

Our topic for this circle session is a very useful one because it gives us a chance to talk about things we do that help us get rid of stress and enjoy life. It's also going to allow us to pick up some good tips from each other on how to be our own best friend. The topic is, "Something I Do for My Own Well-Being."

Most of us find ways to be good to ourselves, but with all the stress each one of us has to deal with, the more ideas we can get for managing stress, the better. Think about things you do for yourself to be healthy, to relax, play, or feel good in general. Perhaps you have a special time when you go off alone to think calmly and take in pleasant surroundings. Maybe you have a form of exercise you do that helps you get rid of tension and allows you to rest very well afterward. You may enjoy losing yourself in some kind of creative activity that relieves built-up stress. Whatever it is, we'd enjoy hearing about it. The topic is, "Something I Do for My Own Well-Being. "

Discussion Questions:

1. Who has the most influence on how well or how poorly you manage your stress levels?
2. What similarities did you notice in the methods that were mentioned?
3. What new ideas did you get for managing stress?

Additional Sharing Circle Topics

Something That Causes Me Stress
I Was So Distressed I Got Sick
I Did Something for My Body and It Improved My Spirit
Something I Worried About That Turned Out Okay
What I Do When the Going Gets Tough
I Problem I'm Trying to Solve
Someone I Can Talk to When I'm Worried
My Favorite Physical Exercise
Where I Go When I Want to Be Alone
A Way I Take Care of My Body
What I Say When I Talk to Myself
A Way I've Learned to Calm Myself Down
Music That Makes Me Feel Good
A Time I Felt Upset and Didn't Know Why

Self-Concept

Activities in this unit teach students to:

- identify their unique abilities and talents and explain how those contribute to group success.

- recognize themselves for their accomplishments, and understand how accomplishments affect their feelings and self-concept.

- understand the nature of self-talk, the effects of positive and negative self-talk, and specific ways to control inner dialogue.

Sharing Circles in this unit allow students to:

- describe an activity they enjoy primarily for the feelings of accomplishment it provides, and discuss how accomplishments contribute to a positive self-concept.

- identify the role or situation in which they most like themselves and have the strongest self-concept.

We All Have Talents
Writing, Sharing, and Discussion

Objectives:

The students will:

— describe their unique abilities and talents.

— acknowledge the abilities and talents of classmates.

— demonstrate understanding of the concept, "strength in diversity."

Materials:

one copy of the experience sheet, "My Special Gifts and Talents," and writing materials for each student

Procedure:

Introduce the activity by asking the students to think about talents or "gifts" that they possess. Explain that a talent or gift is a special ability, like the ability to play a musical instrument or to draw pictures, or speak another language. Some people have a talent for math, science, or history; others are gifted at making friends or playing a particular sport. A gift or talent can be almost anything a person does well. Describe to the students two or three gifts or talents that you possess.

Distribute the experience sheet, "My Special Gifts and Talents." Have the students record their name at the top of the sheet, and then write down as many of their own gifts/talents as they can think of. While the students are working, circulate and offer help and suggestions as needed. Ensure that every child identifies and records several gifts/ talents.

When they have completed their experience sheets, ask the students to look over what they have written, and to circle one talent that they would feel comfortable describing to their classmates. Then have the students form groups of four to six, and take turns sharing their thoughts and feelings about their identified talent. Have the students return to their seats for a general discussion.

Discussion Questions:

1. What is a gift or talent? How can you recognize your own talents?
2. How are our gifts and talents the same? How are they different?
4. What would the world be like if everyone had exactly the same gifts and talents?
5. What would happen if everyone on a football team were a talented passer, but no one had a talent for blocking, kicking, catching, running, or calling plays?
6. How can we use our individual talents and abilities to make our class a better place to learn?

My Special Gifts and Talents
Experience Sheet

I, _____ , bring these special gifts and
talents to my classroom:

1. _____

_____

2. _____

_____

3. _____

_____

4. _____

_____

5. _____

_____

6. _____

_____

7. _____

_____

8. _____

_____

9. _____

_____

10. _____

_____

An Accomplishment I'm Proud Of
Art and Discussion

Objectives:
The students will:
—describe ways in which they can meet personal needs and goals through work.
—describe relationships among ability, effort and achievement.

Materials:
construction paper; watercolors; brushes; pans of water; colored markers or pencils

Procedure:
Introduce the activity. Ask the students what they think an accomplishment is. Record their ideas on the chalkboard. Suggest that an accomplishment can be a special skill or ability acquired by practice and effort, or a goal reached through work. Invite the students to help you make a list of possible accomplishments that someone their age might accrue. Record their suggestions and add some of your own, such as making a good grade in Math, constructing a model at home, hitting a home run in a game, winning a contest or award, learning to make chocolate chip cookies, or training a dog to sit and roll over.

Explain that you want the students to illustrate one of their favorite accomplishments, using watercolors. Ask them to think of an accomplishment or achievement that made them proud. Reread the list from the board to help them remember one that is appropriate.

Distribute the art materials. Suggest that the students either paint themselves achieving a goal or paint a symbol of the achievement, such as a "fastest runner" award. Circulate around the room as the students begin to paint. Offer encouragement to students who are reticent to think of personal accomplishments.

After the paintings are dry, ask each child to use a colored marker to write below the illustration, "I am proud that I..." and name the accomplishment. Invite students to share their pictures with the class. Lead a culminating discussion before posting the paintings on a bulletin board.

Discussion Questions:
1. How difficult was it to think of an accomplishment to illustrate?
2. Why is it important to be aware of our accomplishments?
3. How does accomplishing things contribute to self-esteem?
5. What feelings and sensations do you have inside when you accomplish something?

Extension:
Ask the students to keep a journal or log of their accomplishments during the year. Every time a student does something special in class, like helping someone with a task, getting a good grade on a test, handing in homework on time for a week, showing good sportsmanship, etc., suggest that the student add it to his or her list along with the date. This will enhance self-esteem and remind the students of the many things they accomplish during the school day.

Talking to Yourself
Presentation, Discussion, and Experiment

Objectives:

The students will:

—recognize characteristics of high self-esteem and low self-esteem.

—learn and practice methods of positive self-talk.

—demonstrate understanding of how positive self-talk enhances self-esteem.

Materials:

chalkboard and chalk or chart paper and markers

Procedure:

Ask the students if they know what is meant by the terms self-image and self-esteem. Involve the students in a discussion, making these points about the importance of self-esteem and the role of self-talk in building high self-esteem.

• Self-image is the picture you have of yourself. Self-esteem is how you *feel* about that picture. If you like the picture (the total person, not a photograph or image in the mirror); if it makes you feel strong, powerful, and capable, then you probably have high self-esteem. If you don't like the picture, if makes you feel inferior, powerless, and incapable of doing things well, then you may have low self-esteem. Of course, your self-esteem can be anywhere in between, too.

• Your self-esteem significantly impacts how you behave, learn, relate, work, and play. With high self-esteem, you are poised and confident, have generally good social relationships, are less influenced by peers, and usually make good decisions. With low self-esteem, the reverse is generally true.

• Self-esteem, whether high or low, tends to be self-perpetuating. When you feel good about yourself, you project confidence and people treat you differently than they do when you feel poorly about yourself. Because you are treated well, your positive beliefs about yourself are reinforced and validated and you project even greater confidence, thus perpetuating a positive cycle. Conversely, a negative cycle occurs when you expect and project negative things about yourself.

Over time, if you have high self-esteem, you:

—are proud of your accomplishments.

—tolerate frustrations as they come along.

—take responsibility for your actions.

—approach new challenges with enthusiasm.

—experience a broad range of emotions and feelings.

If you have low self-esteem, you:
—avoid situations and experiences that involve risk.
—down play or belittle your talents as not being good enough.
—blame others for your failings.
—are easily influenced by others.
—feel powerless, and are frequently defensive.
—are easily frustrated.

• Disappointments happen on a daily basis and can affect you for better or worse, depending on how you react to them. How you react is frequently based on how you feel about yourself. When you fail a test in school, if you have high self-esteem, you look at your own responsibility in the failure. You might think you could have studied more, or that next time you will pass, or that it is simply a tough subject for you. If you have low self-esteem and fail a test, you are more likely to blame the teacher or the system and to conclude that you're incapable. Your low self-esteem causes you to draw a false conclusion and verbalize it to yourself by thinking, "I must be stupid," instead of "I feel bad about failing, but it's not the worst thing that could happen. I'll do better next time." Such verbalizations are examples of **SELF-TALK**.

• When you were very young, one of the main ways you developed self-esteem was by paying attention to how your family, teachers, and friends treated you, and how they talked about you. If they liked you and said you were a worthwhile person, then you had good reason to feel the same way about yourself. Today, what others think and say about you is still important, but even more important is what you think about yourself, and what you say to yourself. Now that you're not a child anymore, the most powerful influence on your self-esteem is your own self-talk.

• Be watchful of your self-talk. The more positive your self-talk, the higher your self-esteem, the more negative your self-talk, the lower your self-esteem. If you find yourself saying something negative or seeing the worst possible side of a situation, tell yourself, "Stop!" Discontinue the negative thought and substitute a positive thought.

Describe situations that could lead to negative self-talk. Have volunteers give an example of negative self-talk followed by an example of positive self-talk for each situation:
1. You strike out in a ball game.
2. You find out your parents are divorcing.
3. You get a poor grade in a class.
4. You don't make the team.
5. Your project is eliminated in the second round of judging for the state science fair.
6. You lose in an election for class office.
7. When you and your best friend go places together, he or she always seems to get more attention than you do.
8. You fall down during a dance recital.

Tell the students that for the next four weeks, you want them to work with a partner, consciously practicing the use of positive self-talk. Explain that the partners are to monitor, encourage, and assist each other. They are to act as an extra set of ears, calling attention to negative self-talk and reminding their partner to substitute positive self-talk. Once a week, hold a 10-minute debriefing period and ask partners to evaluate their progress.

At the end of the 4 weeks, facilitate a follow-up discussion.

Discussion Questions:

1. How does self-talk affect self-esteem?
2. Why is it important to build your self-esteem?
3. Under what circumstances did you tend to use negative self-talk?
4. When did you have difficulty using positive self-talk?
5. What strategies did you use to help your partner? How can you use those strategies to help yourself?

Something I Enjoy Doing Because It Gives Me a Feeling of Accomplishment
A Sharing Circle

Objectives:

The students will:

—name an activity they engage in because of the feelings of accomplishment it generates.

—give themselves credit for one or more accomplishments.

Introduce the Topic:

Our topic today is about the pleasure we get from accomplishing things. Sometimes that pleasure is enough to bring us back again and again to the same activity. So let's talk about, "Something I Enjoy Doing Because It Gives Me a Feeling of Accomplishment."

Perhaps you like the challenge of playing chess. You don't win every time, but when you do you feel so great that you can't wait to play another game. Maybe you get similar feelings from tennis, painting, developing computer programs, surfing the WEB, fixing dinner for your family, or helping your dad fix things around home. The thing you share doesn't have to be big and impressive, just something that causes you to feel proud — that motivates you to repeat the experience. Think about it for a few moments. The topic is, "Something I Enjoy Doing Because It Gives Me a Feeling of Accomplishment."

Discussion Questions:

1. What motivates you to do the thing you described, the actual activity or the feelings you get from doing the activity?
2. What feelings and sensations do you experience when you accomplish something?
3. How do accomplishments build your self-esteem?

When I Like Myself Most
A Sharing Circle

Objectives:

The students will:

—describe positive characteristics about themselves.

—demonstrate positive attitudes about themselves.

State the Topic.

Today, we are going to have a chance to say something positive about ourselves — something we like and respect in ourselves. The topic is, "When I Like Myself Most."

What is it that you like most about yourself. Perhaps you feel best about yourself when you know you are learning something easily at school. Maybe you like yourself most when you are drawing a picture, playing soccer, or working on a group project. Do you like yourself when you are helpful to another person or kind to an animal? Or do you like yourself most when you are having fun with your friends? Why not close your eyes and think about it for a moment or two. Raise your hand when you are ready to share. The topic is, "When I Like Myself Most."

Discussion Questions:

1. Why is it so important to like ourselves?
2. If you know when you like yourself most, can you cause those times to happen?
3. When you are feeling very good about yourself, do others like you better too? Why?

Additional Sharing Circle Topics

What People Like About Me
Something I'm Good At
I Did Something That Made Me Feel Like a Good Person
Something I Did or Made That I'm Proud Of
Something I Accomplished That Really Pleased Me
A Time I Made a Big Effort and Succeeded
A Time I Knew I Could Do It
Something About Me That's Special
Something I Like About Myself
Something I Wish I Could Do Better
A Success I Recently Experienced
A Time I Won and Loved It
A Time I Lost and Took It Hard
First I Imagined It, Then I Created It
When Someone Expected the Very Best of Me
My Greatest Asset

Personal Responsibility

Activities in this unit teach students to:

- accept personal responsibility for things they "have" to do.

- understand and experience four components of responsibility: accountability, excellence, self-control and graceful winning and losing (being a good sport).

- distinguish between responsible and irresponsible alternatives in real conflict situations experienced by their peers, and clarify what constitutes responsible behavior.

Sharing Circles in this unit allow students to:

- describe incidents in which they defended a belief or conviction.

- identify at least one responsible habit that they have developed.

Have to...Choose to...
An Exercise in Accepting Responsibility

Objectives:

The students will:

—contrast the attitude of being compelled to do something with the attitude of choosing to do it.

—describe feelings associated with taking responsibility for their actions.

Materials:

one copy of the experience sheet, "Have to... Choose to..." for each student

Procedure:

Often students express the belief that they have little choice concerning their day-to-day activities. They point to the expectations of parents, teachers, and "the system" as justification for this belief. Some students feel victimized and powerless. This activity gives students an opportunity to recognize that they do have choices, and to understand how negative self-talk undermines their power and control.

Distribute the experience sheets. Instruct the students to create a list of things they feel they *have to* do, such as homework, chores, going to school, etc.

Have the students pair up and read their list to a partner.

Next, tell the students to draw a line through the word "have" in each statement and write the word "choose" in its place. Instruct the students to read the list to their partner again.

Expect disagreements concerning what the students *have to do* and what they *choose to do*. Ask what consequences they would face if they didn't do some of the things they listed. Point out that they choose to do many things in order to avoid these consequences. When the students recognize that at some level they are indeed choosing their actions, they will experience a greater sense of control in their lives.

In the spaces at the bottom of the activity sheet, have the students write in some positive self-talk statements describing their freedom of choice. For example, "I freely choose every action I take," or "No one forces me to do anything. I am responsible for my choices."

Lead a culminating discussion.

Discussion Questions:

1. How do your feelings differ when you say "I choose to..." from when you say, "I have to..." in talking about your responsibilities?
2. How much of a choice do you really have about the things you listed?
3. What have you learned about responsibility from this activity?

Have to...Choose to
Experience Sheet

Make a list of things you think you have to do. Be as specific as possible.

Examples:
I have to do my math homework.
I have to take out the trash at home.
I have to arrive at school before 8:00 a.m..

1. I have to _____

2. I have to _____

3. I have to _____

4. I have to _____

5. I have to _____

6. I have to _____

7. I have to _____

8. I have to _____

9. I have to _____

10. I have to _____

Positive self-talk statements:

1. _____

_____

2. _____

_____

3. _____

_____

Responsibility Log
Self-Assessment

Objectives:

The students will:

—explain what it means to be responsible.

—relate specific examples of responsible behavior.

—monitor and describe in writing their responsible and irresponsible behaviors for a prescribed period.

Materials:

two or more copies of the "Responsibility Log" for each student; chalkboard and chalk

Procedure:

Begin by discussing the meaning of the word *responsibility*. List the following four components of responsibility on the board and ask the students to think of <u>specific examples</u> that might fit under each one. (Nonspecific examples are listed below in the form of do's and don'ts.) Invite the students to share incidents from their own experience.

Accountability

• Think before you act.

• Before you make a decision or take an action, think about how it will affect the other people involved. What will be the consequences?

• When you do something wrong or make a mistake, admit it and accept the consequences. Don't blame others or make excuses.

• Don't take credit for the achievements of others.

• Do what you should do, or have agreed to do, even if it is difficult.

Excellence

• Set a good example in everything you do.

• Do your best.

• Don't quit — keep trying.

• Make it your goal to always be proud of your performance (schoolwork, homework, projects, completed chores, athletic or other performances, etc.)

Self-control or self-restraint

• Always control yourself.

• Control your temper — don't throw things, scream, hit others or use bad language.

• Wait your turn.

• Show courtesy and good manners.

Being a good sport

• Win and lose with grace.

• Don't brag when you win or complain and make excuses when you lose.

• Take pride in how you play the game, not just whether you win.

Continue the discussion until the students understand the meaning of responsibility and many specific examples of responsible behavior have been shared. Then announce that, for the next few days, the students are going to keep logs describing actions that are clearly responsible and clearly not responsible.

Distribute the "Responsibility Log" and go over the directions with the students. Explain that the students should write down actions that they know *are* responsible (doing their best on a homework assignment and completing it on time; admitting when they forget to do a chore; congratulating the other team when they lose a game, etc.) as well as actions they feel are *not* responsible (not paying attention in class, blaming another person, procrastinating on an assignment, etc.).

Announce a date when the completed logs are due. Allow from 2 to 5 days, depending on the maturity of your students. Commend (for their responsibility) those students who complete the logs on time.

Before collecting the logs, have the students share their results in groups of four. Finally, lead a culminating class discussion.

Discussion Questions:

1. Which do you have more of, actions which are responsible or actions which are not responsible?
2. What surprised you about the results of your log?
3. How do you feel when you take a responsible action? How do you feel when your actions are not responsible?
4. In which area of responsibility do you think you need to improve?

Responsibility Log
Experience Sheet

For the next few days, pay close attention to your actions. Write down things you say and do that are clearly responsible actions. Also, write down things you say and do that you realize are not responsible actions.

Action	Responsible?	Reactions of Others

I Learned _____

Action	Responsible?	Reactions of Others

I Learned _____

Action	Responsible?	Reactions of Others

I Learned _____

Action	Responsible?	Reactions of Others

I Learned _____

Action	Responsible?	Reactions of Others

I Learned _____

Action	Responsible?	Reactions of Others

I Learned _____

Action	Responsible?	Reactions of Others

I Learned _____

Action	Responsible?	Reactions of Others

I Learned _____

Action	Responsible?	Reactions of Others

I Learned _____

How Would You Handle This Situation Responsibly?
Writing and Discussion

Objectives:

The students will:

—describe a personal experience involving the issue of responsibility.

—define ethical behavior in relation to real situations.

Materials:

writing materials

Procedure:

Note: This activity requires two or more class sessions.

Begin the first session by asking the students to think of situations they have faced in which it was hard to choose the most responsible thing to do. For example, what do you do when you have made a commitment to participate in a meeting, and something else comes up that is equally important and more attractive to you? Or what do you do when a close friend is involved in something illegal, unethical, or dangerous? Discuss a few examples, including one from your own experience.

Ask the students to write about one personal experience of this nature, without putting their names on their stories. Allow plenty of time to complete the writing in class, or assign it as homework.

Collect the completed stories. Read all of the stories and select four or five to review aloud in the second class session. The best kinds of stories to select are ones that:

• reflect typical binds that the students can relate to.

• provide sufficiently detailed information to give the reader/listener most or all pertinent facts.

Begin the second session by reading one of the stories. Emphasize that the identity of the student who wrote the story is not important.

Have the class brainstorm possible ways — either responsible or irresponsible — to handle the situation described in the story. Write all suggestions on the chalkboard.

On a second chalkboard, list ideas concerning what constitutes responsible and irresponsible behavior. Ask the students to forget the story for a minute or two, and just think about behavior in general. In this discussion, be sure to refer to:

1. the rights of individuals to meet their own needs.
2. the importance of not harming others.
3. standards of honesty, integrity, and ethical behavior
4. how such values and beliefs can be reconciled when they appear to conflict.

Return to the suggestions for handling the situation described in the story. Ask the students which are responsible and which are not. Circle the suggestions that the students generally agree are responsible. Follow this procedure with the other stories you have selected. You may wish to spread this over several class sessions.

Conduct an informal discussion, asking the students to share recent personal experiences in which they consciously pondered alternatives before doing what seemed best.

Discussion Questions:

1. How do you resolve an ethical dilemma like the ones some of us described? What process do you use?
2. Do you tend to look at each situation individually, or do you always apply certain basic standards? Explain.
3. How do you feel when your decision violates your own ethical standards?

A Time I Stood Up for Something I Strongly Believe In
A Sharing Circle

Objectives:

The students will:

—describe and take credit for situations in which they demonstrated the courage of their convictions.

—describe what it feels like to take an unpopular public position.

Introduce the Topic:

Today's topic is, "A Time I Stood Up for Something I Strongly Believe In." Most of us have probably experienced at least once the necessity to take a stand concerning something. Standing up for a belief can be difficult, especially if friends or relatives do not agree with us. Even when they do agree, it is not necessarily easy to state our beliefs publicly. Think of a time when this happened to you.

Maybe you saw others doing something that you felt was wrong, and you confronted them. Perhaps you were involved in a discussion about a controversial subject, and you stated your views, even though they were unpopular. You may remember being nervous and worrying about the uncertainty of the situation. Or you may have felt very sure of yourself. Perhaps when you look back on the occasion, you recall a sense of pride, accomplishment, or even daring. If the outcome was different from what you wanted, tell us what you learned from the experience. Remember, don't mention any names. The topic is, "A Time I Stood Up for Something I Strongly Believe In."

Discussion Questions:

1. What similarities were there in our reasons for standing up for what we believe in?
2. When is it hardest for you to stand up for your beliefs?
3. What conditions enable you to stand up for what you believe in?

A Responsible Habit I've Developed
A Sharing Circle

Objectives:

The students will:

—describe and take credit for responsible behaviors.

—realize that responsible habits are developed through repeated practice.

Introduce the Topic:

No matter how responsible we already are, we can always learn more about this important value. It's also important to give ourselves credit for the responsible things we do on a regular basis. Our topic for this sharing circle is, "A Responsible Habit I've Developed."

When we do something again and again it becomes a habit. That's how some of our responsible actions become habits. We do them so often we don't even think about them anymore. Do you have any habits like that? Maybe you brush your teeth every day without being reminded, put your dirty clothes in a hamper as soon as you take them off, or pick up things you see lying around the house. Perhaps you feed and exercise a pet regularly, make your bed as soon as you get up in the morning, or check every weekend to see if you can do anything to assist an elderly neighbor. Or maybe you always finish your homework before watching TV, or your yard chores before going off to play on Saturday. Think it over and tell us about a responsible action that you do regularly. Our topic is, "A Responsible Habit I've Developed."

Discussion Questions:

1. How does having a responsible habit make you feel about yourself?
2. Can you simply decide to develop a habit and then do it? Why or why not?
3. How are habits developed?
4. What responsible habits did you hear about today that you would like to develop, too?

Additional Sharing Circle Topics

A Time I Kept My Promise
How I Help at School
How I Show That I'm a Good Citizen
How I Show Respect Toward Others
A Time I Helped Without Being Asked
A Promise That Was Hard to Keep
I Admitted That I Did It
I Faced a Problem on My Own
I Told the Truth and Was Glad
I Kept an Agreement
A Way in Which I'm Responsible
A Time I Did Something to Help the Community
What I Wish I Could Do to Make This a Better World
People Seem to Respect Me When...
Someone Tried to Make Me Do Something I Didn't Want to Do
I Do My Best in School When...
A Time I Said "No" to Peer Pressure
A Way I Changed to Be a Better Friend
A Rule We Have in My Family
I Said Yes When I Wanted to Say No
A Time I Had the Courage of My Convictions
My Favorite Excuse
A Responsibility I Have at Home
A Time Someone Made a Promise to Me and Kept It
A Time I Didn't Keep My Promise
I Took a Positive Attitude Toward One of My Responsibilities
A Task I Didn't Like at First, But Do Like Now
An Irresponsible Habit I've Decided to Drop
A Responsible Habit I Plan to Have as an Adult

Empathy

Activities in this unit teach students to:

- identify various feelings by carefully observing the nonverbal behaviors of others.

- listen actively to another person, demonstrating empathy and accurate understanding.

- develop empathy as a basis for offering advice to someone with a problem.

Sharing Circles in this unit allow students to:

- identify incidents in which they took the perspective of another person and discuss the effects their empathy had on the situation and/or relationship.

- describe experiences in which they were the recipients of empathy, and discuss they benefits they experienced.

Can You Tell How He or She Feels?
Pantomime and Discussion

Objectives:
The students will:
—demonstrate nonverbal behaviors appropriate to specific feelings.
—correctly identify feelings based on body language, facial expressions, and other nonverbal cues.
——recognize that feelings are conveyed primarily through nonverbal means.

Materials:
descriptions of situations written on small pieces of paper, folded and placed in a container — one description for every two students. The descriptions should portray a variety of emotion-producing situations, like: "You just got a new puppy and your friend is very jealous." or "You and your friend are walking down a dark street at night. Suddenly, you hear a strange noise, but your friend doesn't hear it and thinks you are making it up."

Procedure:
Ask the students to pair up. Have each pair draw one sheet of paper with a situation written on it. Direct each pair to go off to a private place for five minutes and plan a short pantomime of the situation. Explain that the students are to act only with their faces and bodies. They may neither say words, nor make vocal noises. The object is to do such a good job of acting that the class will be able to tell how each actor is feeling in his/her role. If the class can guess the situation, that's fine, but it is not necessary.

When the students have finished planning, have them enact their pantomimes one pair at a time. Enjoy each pantomime and applaud when it is over.

After each pantomime, ask the class to tell the actors how they appeared to be feeling in their roles. Finally, ask the actors to describe the situation they were acting out. Lead a summary discussion.

Discussion Questions:
1. Do our bodies and faces have a language of their own?
2. What did you learn about that language through this activity?
3. How much empathy did you feel for the actors? What enabled you to feel empathy?
4. How do people reveal their emotions — mostly through their words or mostly through their facial expressions and body language?
5. If you want to really empathize with someone, what should you pay close attention to?

The Active Listener
Communication Skill Practice

Objectives:

The students will:

—define the role of the receiver in communication.

—identify and demonstrate "active listening" behaviors.

Materials:

a diagrammatic model of the communications process (see below) drawn on the chalkboard or chart paper; a list of topics written on the chalkboard (see below); one copy of the experience sheet, "Be an Active Listener!" for each student

Procedure:

On the chalkboard or chart paper, draw a simple diagram illustrating the communication process. For example, print the words, **SENDER** and **RECEIVER** and draw two arrows — one going in each direction — between the two words. Explain to the students that in order for two people to enjoy and encourage each other, to work, play, or solve problems together, they need to be able to communicate effectively. In your own words, say: *In every example of communication, no matter how small, a message is sent from one person (the sender) to the other person (the receiver). The message is supposed to tell the receiver something about the feelings and/or thoughts of the sender. Because the sender cannot "give" the receiver his or her feelings and thoughts, they have to be "coded" in words. Good communicators pick words that describe their feelings and thoughts as closely as possible. Nonverbal "signals" almost* *always accompany the verbal message; for example, a smile, a frown, or a hand gesture. Sometimes the entire message is nonverbal. Good communicators send nonverbal signals that exactly match their feelings and thoughts.*

Ask the students to describe what a good receiver says and does to show that s/he is interested in what the sender is saying and is really listening. Write their ideas on the chalkboard. Be sure to include these behaviors:

1. Face the sender.
2. Look into the sender's eyes.
3. Be relaxed, but attentive.
4. Listen to the words and try to picture in your own mind what the sender is saying.
5. Don't interrupt or fidget. When it is your turn to respond, don't change the subject or start telling your own story.
6. If you don't understand something, wait for the sender to pause and then ask, "What do you mean by..."
7. Try to feel what the sender is feeling (show empathy).
8. Respond in ways that let the sender know that you are listening and understand what is being said. Ways of responding might include nodding, saying "uh huh," or giving feedback that proves you are listening, for example:
    - **Briefly summarize:** "You're saying that you might have to quit the team in order to have time for a paper route."
    - **Restate feelings, showing empathy:** "You must be feeling pretty bad." or "You sound really happy!"

Tell the students that this type of listening is called *active listening*. Ask them if they can explain why the word *active* is used to describe it.

Ask the students to form groups of three. Tell them to decide who is **A**, who is **B**, and who is **C**. Announce that you are going to give the students an opportunity to practice active listening. Explain the process:

*In the first round, **A** will be the sender and **B** will be the receiver and will use active listening. **C** will be the observer. **C**'s job is to notice how well **B** listens, and report his/her observations at the end of the round. I will be the timekeeper. We will have three rounds, so that you can each have a turn in all three roles. When you are the sender, pick a topic from the list on the board, and remember to pause occasionally so that your partner can respond.*

Signal the start of the first round. Call time after 3 minutes. Have the observers give feedback for 1 minute. Tell the students to switch roles. Conduct two more rounds. Lead a follow-up discussion. Distribute the experience sheet and suggest that the students keep it in their notebooks and refer to it from time to time.

Discussion Questions:

1. How did it feel to "active listen?"
2. How difficult was it to feel empathy for your partner?
3. What was it like to be the observer?
4. When you were the sender, how did you feel having someone really empathize with and listen to you?
5. What was easiest about active listening? What was hardest?
6. What did you learn from your observer?
7. Why is it important to learn to be a good listener?

List of topics:

"A Time I Needed Some Help"
"Something I'd Like to Do Better"
"A Problem I Need to Solve"
"A Time I Got Into an Argument"
"A Time I Had to Make a Tough Decision"
"Something I'd Like to Be or Do When I'm an Adult"

Be an Active Listener!
Experience Sheet

Listening is a very important part of good communication. Listed below are characteristics of a good listener. Check the ones that describe you most of the time.

A good listener:

___ Faces the speaker.

___ Looks into the speaker's eyes.

___ Is relaxed, but attentive.

___ keeps an open mind.

___ Listens to the words and tries to picture what the speaker is saying.

___ Doesn't interrupt or fidget.

___ Waits for the sender to pause to ask clarifying questions.

___ Tries to feel what the sender is feeling (feels and shows empathy).

___ Nods and says "uh huh," or summarizes to let the speaker know he/she is listening.

What are your two strongest qualities as a listener?

1._____

_____

_____

2._____

_____

_____

What is your weakest quality as a listener?

_____

_____

_____

What are three things you can do to become a better listener?

1._____

_____

_____

2._____

_____

_____

3._____

_____

_____

Dear Matilda . . .
Creative Writing and Discussion

Objectives:
The students will:
—write about a real problem.
—attempt to empathize with and describe possible solutions to someone else's problem.

Materials:
paper, a collection box (for problems), and bulletin boards for posting letters and responses

Procedure:
Read aloud a newspaper column to which readers write with problems and in which the columnist offers advice and solutions.

Ask the students to write a brief letter to "Matilda." Assure them that Matilda will respond. Explain that the letter should consist of a request for advice concerning a real problem, present or past. Urge the students to include enough facts and clues as to the emotions of the people involved to allow someone reading the letter to empathize with their feelings and point of view. If the students can't think of a problem of their own to describe, tell them its okay to describe someone else's problem, as long as they know enough about it to be specific. Ask the students to sign their letters with fictitious names, and drop them into the collection box.

Have each student reach into the box and draw out a letter. Instruct the students to prepare an answer to the letter. Allow the students to consult with each other in dyads or triads to generate ideas for thoughtful, empathic responses. The rest of the period can be devoted to writing. Ask the students to sign their real names to their response.

Collect and read the letters and responses. Correct the responses only, and offer the students an opportunity rewrite them. Have the students post their letters and responses on a class bulletin board. Give the students time to circulate and read each other's letters and responses.

Discussion Questions:
1. What was hardest about this assignment? What was easiest?
2. How much empathy did you, as "Matilda," feel for your correspondent in the situation s/he described?
3. What kinds of questions did you, as "Matilda," want to ask your correspondent?
4. How did lack of personal contact affect your ability to empathize with the situation?

A Time I Put Myself in Someone Else's Shoes
A Sharing Circle

Objectives:

The students will:

—describe instances of perspective-taking

—explain how perspective taking contributes to interpersonal understanding and problem solving.

Introduce the Topic:

Our topic for this session is, "A Time I Put Myself in Someone Else's Shoes." Do you know what that expression means? Putting yourself in someone else's shoes means seeing and feeling things from that person's point of view. Think of a time when you tried very hard to understand how someone was thinking or feeling by imagining what it would be like to be in that person's shoes. Maybe you had a conflict with a friend and tried to see the conflict the way he did. Or maybe you wanted to better understand how a situation looked to someone from a different culture, so you asked questions and listened carefully to that person's answers. Have you ever tried to understand what it would be like to be blind, or to have some other kind of disability? Have you ever tried to understand how someone feels who cannot speak your language? Taking the perspective of another people helps us to understand or <u>empathize</u> with that person. Tell us what you learned by walking in someone else's shoes. Our topic is, "A Time I Put Myself in Someone Else's Shoes."

Discussion Questions:

1. How did it feel to put yourself in someone else's shoes?
2. What do you need to do in order to understand another person's point of view?
3. How does empathizing with others help us solve problems and resolve conflicts?
4. How do you feel when a person refuses to understand where you are coming from?
5. What would the world be like if people and countries were unwilling to understand each other's points of view?

I Didn't Say a Word, But They Knew How I Felt
A Sharing Circle

Objectives:

The students will:

—recall a time when someone empathized with them by accurately reading nonverbal cues.

—recognize that feelings are conveyed primarily through nonverbal means.

—describe how it feels to gain someone's empathy and understanding.

Introduce the Topic:

Our topic for today is, "I Didn't Say a Word, But They Knew How I Felt." We've talked about empathy— about being able to determine the feelings of others without their telling us. In this circle, think of a time when another person, or a group of people, knew how you were feeling, even though you didn't tell them. Maybe you were disappointed, joyful, embarrassed, confused, angry, or thrilled. Whatever the feeling was, someone could see it in you, and told you so. Someone empathized with your feelings. Take a few minutes to think of such a time. The topic is, "I Didn't Say a Word, But They Knew How I Felt."

Discussion Questions:

1. How do you think the others knew what you were feeling?
2. How did you feel when someone empathized with your feelings?
3. How do you feel when someone refuses to empathize, or even understand, your feelings though you've made them very clear?

Additional Sharing Circle Topics

A Time When I Accepted Someone Else's Feelings
Someone Didn't Say a Word, But I Knew How S/he Felt
A Time I Showed Someone That I Cared
A Time I Felt Sorry for Someone Who Was Put Down
I Helped Someone Who Needed and Wanted My Help
A Time I Listened Well to Someone
Someone Who Always Understands Me
A Person I Can Share My Feelings With
How I Show Someone That I Understand
A Time I Could Have Shown That I Cared, But Didn't
A Time I Failed to Listen to Someone
A Time Someone Really Listened to Me
A Time Someone Failed to Listen to Me
One of the Most Caring People I Know
A Time Someone Understood My Point of View
A Time My Point of View Was Misunderstood

Communication

Activities in this unit teach students to:

- recognize and avoid and/or deal with habits and behaviors that tend to block effective communication.

- listen carefully and interpret information accurately.

- use I-statements to express feelings and thoughts, particularly as an effective alternative to blaming.

Sharing Circles in this unit allow students to:

- explore ingredients of good communication.

- examine behaviors that result in misleading or garbled communication, discuss their consequences, and identify ways of ensuring clear communication.

Identifying Blocks to Communication
Role-Play and Discussion

Objectives:

The students will:

—demonstrate common ways of responding to another person that may block communication.

—describe how different ways of responding may affect a speaker.

—discuss what constitutes effective and ineffective communication.

Materials:

one copy of the experience sheet, "Communication Blockers" for each student; chalkboard and chalk or chart paper and magic marker

Procedure:

Write the following list on the board or chart paper for the students to see when they enter class:

- Interrupting
- Challenging/Accusing/Contradicting
- Dominating
- Judging
- Advising
- Interpreting
- Probing
- Criticizing/Name-calling/Put-downs

Begin the activity by asking the students to think of a heading or title for the list on the board. Write their suggestions down and discuss each one briefly. Add the suggested title, "Communication Blockers," and ask the students if they can imagine how these behaviors might have the effect of hampering communication — or blocking it altogether.

Ask the students to help you role-play each behavior to see what effect it does have on communication. Invite a volunteer to start a conversation with you. Explain that he or she may talk about anything that comes to mind, and should attempt to continue the conversation as long as possible, or until you call time.

As the student begins to speak, respond with one of the communication blockers from the list. Use appropriate gestures, volume, and tone, and make your response as convincing as possible. Continue using examples of that particular communication blocker until (1) the student gives up talking, or (2) the point has been sufficiently made.

After each demonstration, lead a class discussion about the effects of that communication behavior. Ask the discussion questions listed at the end of these directions and others suggested by the demonstration. The following elaboration on the communication stoppers includes suggestions for conducting each demonstration, as well as important points to make during discussion.

Interrupting

Demonstration: Butt in time and again as the student talks, with statements about yourself and things that have happened to you. For example, if the student says, "I have a friend named Sue, and...," interrupt with, "Oh, I know her — well, a little. We met the other day when... etc., etc."

Discussion: Point out how frustrating it is to be interrupted, and how futile it is to continue a conversation when interruptions occur over and over. Interrupting is probably the most frequent way in which communication is blocked.

Advising

Demonstration: Give lots of unasked-for advice. Use statements like, "Well, if I were you...," "I think you should...," and "Have you tried..." If the student says, "I have a friend named Sue, and...," respond with, "Sue has a lot of problems. Take my advice and steer clear or her." or "Be careful what you tell Sue. She can't keep a secret for three minutes." Etc.

Discussion: By giving unsolicited advice, a person immediately assumes a position of superiority. Advice-giving says, "I know better than you do." Advice may also cause the speaker to feel powerless to control his or her own life.

Judging

Demonstration: Evaluate the student and everything he or she says. For example, if the student says, "I have a friend named Sue, and...," say, "Yeah, Sue's part of that stuck-up snob crowd." If the student says, "I want to see that new Hanks movie." say, "Don't waste your money, it's lousy."

Discussion: Judging retards communication even when the judgment is positive. Not only does the "judge" assume a superior position, his or her evaluations may so completely contradict the speaker's own feelings that a contest or argument ensues — or further communication seems pointless.

Interpreting

Demonstration: Analyze everything the student says in order to reveal its "deeper meaning." If the student says, "I have a friend named Sue, and...," say, "You think having Sue as a friend will improve your popularity." If the student denies the desire to be popular, say, "That's just because you have a low self-image."

Discussion: Interpreting and analyzing say that the listener is unwilling to accept the speaker (or the speaker's statements) at face value. Not to mention that the interpretation is frequently wrong.

Dominating

Demonstration: Take over the conversation. If the student says, "I have a friend named Sue, and...," jump in with, "I know Sue's brother. He is..., and not only that, he..., and so..., because..., blah, blah, blah, etc., etc., ad nauseam.

Discussion: We all know how frustrating and annoying it is to be in a conversation with someone who always has something better and more interesting to say than we do. In addition, when one person dominates a conversation, others are forced to use another communication stopper, interrupting, just to get a word in.

Probing

Demonstration: Ask question after question in a demanding tone. If the student says, "I have a friend named Sue, and...," ask, "Why do you hang out with her?" As soon as the student begins to answer, ask, "How long have you known her?" "Is her hair naturally curly?" And so on.

Discussion: Probing tends to put the speaker on the defensive by asking him or her to justify or explain every statement. More importantly, questions may lead the speaker away from what she or he originally wanted to say. The questioner thus controls the conversation and its direction.

Challenging/Accusing/ Contradicting

Demonstration: Contradict what the student says and accuse him or her of being wrong. For example, if the student says, "I have a friend named Sue, and...," say, "She's not really your friend. You know her because she's Anna's friend." If the student says, "Sue and I have a lot in common." say, "You're

dreaming. Name one thing!"

Discussion: Contradictions and accusations put the speaker on the spot, and make it necessary for her or him to take a defensive position. They also say to the speaker, "You are wrong." or "You are bad."

Criticizing/Name-calling/ Putting-down

Demonstration: Make sarcastic, negative remarks in response to everything the student says. If the student says, "I have a friend named Sue, and...," say, "You jerk, what are you hanging out with her for." If the student says, "Because I like her..." respond, "You never did have good sense."

Discussion: Criticism diminishes the speaker. Few of us want to continue a conversation in which we are being diminished. Name-calling and put-downs are frequently veiled in humor, but may nonetheless be hurtful and damaging to a relationship.

Discussion Questions:

1. How did you (the speaker) feel?
2. What effect does this type of response have on the speaker? ...on the conversation? ...on the relationship?
3. How do communication blockers contribute to conflict?
4. Has this ever happened to you? What did you say and/or do?
5. Under what circumstances would it be okay to respond like this?

Communication Blockers
Experience Sheet

Have you ever tried to have a conversation with someone who wouldn't let you finish a sentence? Have you ever attempted to discuss a problem with someone who had an answer for everything? Bad communication habits can stop a conversation short. Here are a few to avoid:

Interrupting

Interruptions are the most common cause of stalled communication. It's frustrating to be interrupted in the middle of a sentence, and when interruptions happen over and over again, talking feels like a waste of time.

Advising

Few people enjoy getting advice they haven't asked for. Statements that begin with, "Well, if I were you......   or "If you ask me......"   are like yellow warning lights. Advice-giving says, "I'm superior. I know better than you do." Advice can also cause a person to feel powerless — as though she can't make a good decision on her own.

Judging

When you tell people that their ideas or feelings are wrong, you are suggesting that you know more than they do. If your ideas are drastically different from theirs, they'll either defend themselves (argue) or give up on the conversation. Even positive judgments like, "You're the smartest student in class," don't work if the person you're talking to doesn't *feel* very smart.

Interpreting

Some people develop a habit of analyzing everything (including statements) to reveal "deeper meanings." When you interpret or analyze, you imply that you are not willing to accept the speaker or the speaker's statements just as they are. Analyzing is for psychiatrists and counselors, and a lot of the time even they are wrong!

Dominating

We all know how frustrating and annoying it is to be in a conversation with someone who always has something better and more interesting to say than we do. In addition, when you dominate a conversation, others are forced to use another communication blocker — interrupting — just to get a word in.

Probing

Asking a lot of questions ("Why did you go there?" "Who did you see?" "What did he do?") may put the speaker on the defensive by requiring her to explain every statement. More importantly, your questions may lead the speaker *away* from what she originally wanted to say. If you ask too many questions, you are controlling, not sharing, the conversation.

Challenging/Accusing/Contradicting

There's nothing more frustrating than trying to talk with someone who challenges everything you say, insists that your ideas are wrong, or states that what happened was your fault. Contradictions and accusations put the speaker on the spot, and make the speaker defensive.

Criticizing/Name-calling/Put-downs

Don't make sarcastic or negative remarks in response to the things someone says. Criticism whittles away at self-esteem. Hardly anyone wants to continue a conversation that's making him feel bad or small. Even name-calling and put-downs that sound funny can still be hurtful. In the long run, they damage friendships.

Listening to Directions
A Communications Experiment

Objectives:

The students will:
—practice effective listening in situations involving one-way communication.
—test their ability to hear and follow directions accurately.

Materials:

paper and pencils; chalkboard and chalk

Procedure:

Begin by asking the students: How do you know when someone is listening to you?

Accept all responses, jotting ideas on the board. For example, the listener usually:
— looks at me
— is quiet
— shows understanding
— asks questions that make sense
— doesn't interrupt

Point out that, while conversations are an example of two-way communication, there are also many times when communication is mostly one-way. Some of them are very important. Ask the students to help you think of examples of one-way communication in which good listening is very important. Generate a list that includes such instances as:
—when you are lost and ask for directions
—when your teacher gives an assignment
—when your parents tell you where and when to meet them
—when someone is teaching you a new skill
—when the operator is giving you a phone number
—when the principal is explaining a change in schedule over the intercom

Announce that the students are going to see how good they are at listening to one-way communication. Tell them to start right now by listening carefully to your instructions.

Distribute paper and pencils. Tell the students that they have 1 minute to draw a simple design using a circle, a triangle, a rectangle, one curved line, and two straight lines. Write a list of the elements on the board. Tell the students to arrange the elements any way they wish in any size they wish.

When the students have finished, tell them to fold their drawings to hide them from view, and form a dyad with one other person. In your own words, explain the task:

*First decide who is **A** and who is **B**. Then turn your desks or chairs and sit back to back. When it is your turn to be the speaker, you will open your drawing and slowly and clearly describe it to your partner. Your partner will attempt to duplicate the drawing on the back of his or her own sheet. When you are the listener, do not speak or turn around, just listen and draw. You will have 2 minutes to complete the drawing. When I call time, switch roles. Repeat the process for another 2 minutes. The **A**'s will be the first speakers.*

Clarify and answer questions. Then start the exercise, keeping time and signaling the students to switch roles after 2 minutes. When both rounds are completed, tell the partners to turn around and compare their drawings. Urge them to comment on each other's effectiveness as speaker and listener.

Lead a follow-up discussion.

Discussion Questions:
1. What was the hardest part about this exercise? What was the easiest part?
2. What was it like when you were the speaker?
3. What role does listening play in following directions?
4. What kinds of things can happen as a result of poor listening?
5. What kinds of things make it hard to understand directions and other kinds of one-way communication?
6. What should you do if you don't understand?

Variations:
Use the same activity to focus on speaking skills — or both speaking and listening skills. Brainstorm and discuss the process of sending messages clearly and accurately.

Formulating I-Statements
Experience Sheet and Practice Session

Objectives:
The students will:
—practice effectively expressing their thoughts, feelings, and wants.
—compare the use of I-statements to less effective forms of confrontation.

Materials:
one copy of the experience sheet, "Getting Your Message Across," for each student; chalkboard and chalk

Procedure:
Talk to the students about the importance of sending clear, sincere messages to other people. If you have already completed a listening activity with the students, point out that speaking is the other half of the communication process. Emphasize that sending clear messages is particularly important when talking to people who are not good listeners, which unfortunately includes all people some of the time, and many people all of the time. Being heard and understood takes care and effort.

Distribute the experience sheets and go over the first part with the students. Clarify the 6-step process. Ask the students why each step is important and give examples.

1. Ask to be heard.
2. Look directly at the listener.
3. Speak in a clear voice.
4. Use I-statements
5. Check for understanding.
6. Thank the listener

Next, focus on the process for formulating an I-statement. Write the steps as headings across the top of the board. Underneath the headings begin to construct examples. (Use the examples below or think of others that are more relevant.)

• Describe the situation — the person's behavior or the conditions that are causing you a problem.
"When you..."
...interrupt me so much...
...borrow my sweater without asking...
...keep the kitten in your room all the time...
...say things behind my back...
...question me so much...

• State how you feel and how the situation is affecting you.
"I feel...
...frustrated because I can't finish a sentence...
..irritated because the sweater isn't here when I want it...
...sad because I never get to play with her...
...hurt, because you're my friend...
...like you don't trust me.

• Say what you want.
"I'd like you to..."
...listen to me tell my story."
...ask me before you take something."
...share her with me."
...stop talking about me when I'm not around."
...believe me when I tell you something."

Have the students complete the second part of their experience sheet, constructing practice I-statements. Invite several students to read their I-statements to the class. Then involve the students in thinking of other typical situations. Together, develop an I-statement for each one.

Conclude the activity with a summary discussion.

Discussion Questions:

1. What is the most difficult part about sending I-statements?
2. What are some other ways in which people communicate what they want?
3. Why is sending an I-statement more effective than demanding what you want?
4. How do you feel when someone blames or criticizes you?
5. Are you more apt to listen to an I-statement or a blaming, criticizing message? Why?
6. How are you going to use this skill? When are you going to start?

Variations:

Role play some of the situations. Have the actors try less effective ways of communicating their wishes, like demanding, whining, criticizing, name calling, etc., and then substitute an I-statement. Discuss the differences in effectiveness (getting the job done) and the impact on the listener and the relationship (feelings).

Getting Your Message Across
Experience Sheet

When you want to be heard, send a clear message. Follow these steps:

1. Ask to be heard. For example, say, "I'd like to talk to you" or "There's something I want to say."

2. Look directly at the listener.

3. Speak in a clear voice.

4. Use I-Statements. They have three parts:
   - Describe the situation: "When you..."
   - State how you feel: "I feel..."
   - Say what you want: "I'd like you to..."

5. Check for understanding.

6. Thank the listener.

Practice writing some I-statements here:

• You are having a conversation with a friend, but your friend keeps interrupting you. You are getting upset, so you decide to use an I-statement.

When you _____

_____

I feel_____ and I'd like you to _____

_____

_____

• You are trying to study at home. The TV is so loud in the next room that you can't think. You decide to explain how the noise is affecting you.

When you _____

_____

I feel_____ and I'd like you to_____

_____

_____

What I Think
Good Communication Is
A Sharing Circle

Objectives:

The students will:

—describe elements of good communication.

—discuss feelings generated by good and bad communication.

Introduce the Topic:

Today's topic for discussion is, "What I Think Good Communication Is." Communication is an exchange of thoughts, feelings, opinions, or information between two or more people. Today we're going to focus on the ingredients of good communication. There are no right or wrong answers; whatever you contribute will help us develop a better understanding of what's involved. If you like, try thinking about a person with whom you've had particular success communicating and attempt to isolate some of the things that happen during your interactions with that person. Take a few minutes, and then we'll begin sharing on our topic, "What I Think Good Communication Is."

Discussion Questions:

1. What quality or ingredient of good communication was mentioned most often during our sharing?
2. How do you feel after experiencing good communication? ...bad communication?
3. Why is it important to practice good communication?

When What Was Said Was Not What Was Meant
A Sharing Circle

Objectives:

The students will:

—describe instances of insincere communication.

—discuss the benefits of honest communication.

Introduce the Topic:

Today's topic is, "When What Was Said Was Not What Was Meant." I am sure if you think about it, you can remember a time when a person you know said one thing and meant something entirely different. Perhaps a friend said it was okay for you to go to the movies on a night that he or she couldn't go, and later got mad because you did. Or someone expressed liking for your new haircut and later criticized the haircut behind your back. Have teammates or classmates ever gone along with an idea you suggested and then fought it every step of the way? Think for a moment about a time this happened to you, and describe how you handled the situation. When you're ready, we'll begin sharing on the topic, "When What Was Said Was Not What Was Meant."

Discussion Questions:

1. How important is it to say what you mean? Why?
2. Why do people say things they don't mean?
3. How do you feel when you realize that a person's comments were insincere?
4. If you think someone's words are insincere, what can you do?

Additional Sharing Circle Topics

A Time When Listening Would Have Kept Me Out of Trouble
I Told Someone How I Was Feeling
A Time I Listened Well to Someone
Something I See Differently Than My Parents See It
How I Used Sharing Circle Skills Outside the Circle
A Time I Said One Thing But Meant Another
A Time When I Communicated Well
What I Do to Make Myself Understood
A Time When Poor Communication Caused a Misunderstanding
What I Think Poor Communication Is

Group Dynamics

Activities in this unit teach students to:

- distinguish between cooperative and competitive behavior and understand the benefits and limitations of each.

- work together cooperatively to solve a problem, afterwards assessing how their own behaviors and those of others affected the process.

- understand how group efforts are helped and hindered by typical roles that people play in group situations.

Sharing Circles in this unit allow students to:

- describe times when they were excluded from a group, and discuss how it feels to be left out.

- describe positive group experiences, and discuss some of the characteristics of successful groups.

Weighing the Two C's
Stories and Discussion

Objectives:

The students will:

—distinguish between cooperative and competitive behaviors.

—describe the benefits and drawbacks of cooperative and competitive behaviors.

—identify ways that the class can be more cooperative.

Materials:

chalkboard and chalk

Procedure:

Read the following story to the students.

Mr. Monday's class was getting ready for the science fair. The students worked on their projects every day, independently and quietly. First they researched different project ideas. Then they met individually with Mr. Monday to decide what to work on. If a student couldn't come up with an idea, Mr. Monday assigned one. When the students had a question or got stumped, Mr. Monday often sent them to the library to find answers in reference books. Mr. Monday urged the students to keep their projects under wraps and their findings secret, so that everyone would be surprised on the opening day of the fair. The students assembled their displays at home and didn't bring them to school until the day before the fair. Mr. Monday reminded the students that the judges would be awarding prizes for the best entries.

Ms. Friday's class was getting ready for the science fair, too. First, small groups of students researched possible project topics. Then the groups compiled their ideas in one big list and the entire class chose eight projects to work on. The students formed eight teams. Students who weren't sure which team they wanted to belong to were allowed to work on more than one team until they decided. Ms. Friday encouraged all the teams to share ideas with one another. About once a week, she called an "Investigator's Forum" where each team reported on the status of its project, and where everyone offered suggestions and brainstormed ideas to make the projects better. The groups built their displays in class, sometimes staying after school to put in extra time. There was a lot of moving around Ms. Friday's class, and quite a bit of noise, too. Ms. Friday told the students that she wanted all the projects to be the best they could be.

Write the headings "Competitive" and Cooperative" on the chalkboard. Ask the students which label fits Mr. Monday's class and which fits Ms. Friday's class. Then ask them to recall specific attitudes and behaviors in each story that were competitive and cooperative. Write their ideas on the board under the appropriate heading. For example:

Mr. Monday/Competitive
worked alone
kept projects secret
didn't share ideas
concentrated on winning prizes

Ms. Friday/Cooperative
worked in teams
shared ideas
did joint problem solving
talked freely
concentrated to making all projects excellent

Conclude the activity with a total class discussion.

Discussion Questions:

1. What are the benefits of cooperating with others? What are the drawbacks?
2. What are the benefits of competing with others? What are the drawbacks?
3. What activities are competitive and cooperative at the same time? Which approach is more important in those activities? Why?
4. What can this class do to become more cooperative?

Connect!
A Cooperative Team Experience

Objectives:

The students will:

—cooperate in solving a problem.

—identify specific cooperative and competitive behaviors and describe how they affect completion of a team task.

Materials:

construction paper or tag board (one color only) with which to make a set of puzzle pieces for each group of players (see "Preparation," below); table and chairs for each group of players

Preparation:

Start with eight 8-inch by 8-inch squares of construction paper or tag board for each team. Individually cut each square into three to five smaller pieces (see illustration). Place all of the pieces for one team in a single envelope.

Procedure:

If the entire class is playing, ask the students to form teams of five to eight. Have each team sit around a table, and select one member to be its Observer. Announce that all other team members are players.

Take the Observers aside and say to them: *Your job is to stand beside the table while your team is playing the game and notice what happens. Be prepared to describe such*

things as how well the group works together, who shares puzzle parts and who does not; who makes an effort to include everyone and who does not; whether members concentrate only on the puzzle in front of them or watch the progress of all the puzzles; cooperative vs. competitive behaviors; any conflicts that occur and how they are resolved; who provides leadership.

Read aloud the following rules of play:

- Your task is to assemble eight squares of EQUAL size.
- There will be NO talking, pointing, or other nonverbal communication.
- A player may pass puzzle parts to any other team member at any time.
- You may NOT take, ask for, or indicate in any way that you want another team member's puzzle pieces.
- There is no time limit. The game is over when you have finished the task.

Distribute the puzzle pieces randomly among the players. Give each player approximately the same number of pieces.

Give the signal to start play.

At the conclusion of play, have the Observers give feedback to their team. If several teams are playing, have the Observers do this simultaneously. Advise the teams to listen carefully, and not to interrupt, argue with, or put down the Observer.

Discussion Questions:

1. What did you learn from your Observer?
2. What was the object of the game?
3. Which kind of behavior was most effective in this game, cooperative or competitive? Why?
4. What are some of the effects of competitive behavior on a team? ...of cooperative behavior?
5. If anyone emerged as a leader in your group, how did that person demonstrate his or her leadership since there was no talking?
5. If you could play the game again, would you change your own behavior?
6. What did you learn from this experience?

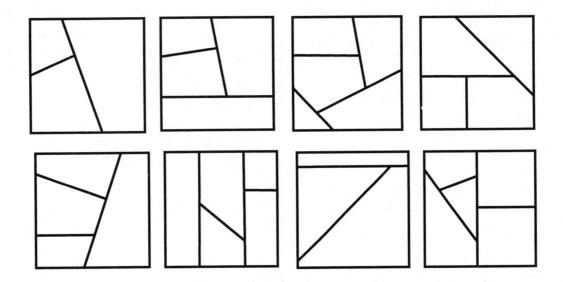

The Spirit Club
A Group Simulation

Objectives:
The students will:
—work as a group to reach a decision.
—describe how roles played by individuals affect group dynamics and task completion.
—identify individual "agendas" and describe how they affect the group.

Materials:
one set on nine 3-inch by 5-inch Role Cards, each printed with a role description (see below)

Procedure:
In advance, print the following role descriptions on the cards:

1. **Information Giver:** You point out facts, ask questions, and give information.
2. **Evaluator:** You encourage the group to talk about the pros and cons of each suggestion. You secretly decide that you will support the idea that is best supported by facts and information.
3. **Clarifier:** You try to make sure everyone understands every idea and suggestion.
4. **Topic Switcher:** You keep getting off the subject.
5. **Facilitator:** You help others participate and suggest ways to share ideas.
6. **Harmonizer:** You try to ease tension and settle any conflicts that occur.
7. **Leader:**   You want to be the leader of the group. To become the leader, you attempt to take charge of the meeting.

8. **Clown:** You get bored, and start telling jokes to try to make the task more fun. You secretly hope the money will be used toward a trip to Disney World.
9. **Dropout:** You think the faculty advisor and school administrators should make the decision. You say so, and then back off.

Choose from ten to fifteen volunteers to participate in the simulation game. Have them move their desks or chairs into a circle near the center of the room. Have the remaining students form an outer circle, and announce that they will be observers. Instruct the observers to take notes so that they can describe what they see to the class in a follow-up discussion. Suggest that they pay attention to both content (what happens) and process (how it happens).

Read the task to the players: *You belong to the Spirit Club here at school. The club sponsors dances and other special events. The club pays for the events it sponsors by selling soft drinks, hot dogs, and snacks at games, concerts, and other school functions. This year, the club has made a lot more money than expected. After all expenses and special events have been paid for, there is still $4,000 left. Your task, as a member of the club, is to decide how the extra money should be used. The club's faculty advisor has said that s/he will support any responsible decision the club makes.*

Randomly distribute the role cards to the players. Tell them to memorize their role and then put the card away or give it back to you. Caution them NOT to divulge their role to other players. If any players have questions about their roles, assist them privately. Instruct those without role cards to play themselves.

Convene the meeting, playing the part of the faculty advisor. Answer any questions the committee members have about the task, and then announce that you have an errand to run and will return in 30 minutes. Take your place among the observers.

At the end of 30 minutes, stop the meeting and lead a debriefing session. Use these and other open-ended questions to debrief the players. Then ask the observers to describe their observations. During any remaining time, facilitate a total class discussion.

Discussion Questions:

1. How did you feel in your role?
2. What problems did you have playing your role?
3. What behaviors were most helpful to the group?
4. What behaviors were least helpful?
5. What would have helped the group reach a decision more easily?
6. How did the "hidden agendas" of some group members affect the process?
7. How was this like real group situations you've experienced?
8. What did you learn from this activity?

Variation:

Design a situation more in keeping with the interests and experiences of your students. The role definitions and discussion questions are generic; only the hidden agenda of the "clown" will need to be modified.

A Time I Felt Left Out
A Sharing Circle

Objectives:

The students will:

—describe feelings associated with being excluded.

—explain that all persons need to belong and to be accepted by others.

Introduce the Topic:

The topic for this session isn't a happy one. It's, "A Time I Felt Left Out." At one time or another, all of us have been left out of something that we wanted to be included in. Maybe it was a game our friends were playing, or a job the family was doing at home, but felt you were too young to participate in. Possibly you weren't feeling well and couldn't go to school on a day everyone else was going on a field trip. Or maybe your friends were invited to a birthday party and you weren't. Whatever it was, you felt left out of what others were doing. Think about it for a few moments and, when you are ready, raise your hand. The topic is, "A Time I Felt Left Out."

Discussion Questions:

1. Why is it so important to us to feel included?
2. What could you have done to be included?
3. What can you do if you see that someone is being left out?

A Time I Worked in a Successful Group
A Sharing Circle

Objectives:

The students will:

—describe characteristics of a successful group.

—describe their contributions to the success of a group.

—state that a successful group needs the diverse abilities of all its members.

Introduce the Topic:

All of us have belonged to a group that has had some form of success. Successful groups have certain characteristics in common. One of these characteristics is interdependence. Interdependence exists when the strength of the group is built on the contributions of its members and the members derive benefits from being part of the group. Today, we are going to look at an experience of our own to explore the characteristic of interdependence. In the process, we're going to discover some other characteristics of successful groups. Our topic is, "A Time I Worked in a Successful Group."

Think of one time when you were a part of a group that achieved something significant. The group might have been a team, or a work group with a particular task to complete. Maybe it was a family group, or a social or religious group. It might even have been a bunch of friends working together. Focus on the group's achievements. What made the group successful? What were some of the characteristics of the group that caused it to function so well? How did you feel when you were part of this group. Take a moment to think about all of these things. The topic is, "A Time I Worked in a Successful Group."

Discussion Questions:

1. How did members of the group feel toward one another?
2. What were some of the contributions that different people made to the success of the groups we discussed?
3. In what ways can groups outperform individuals?
4. Under what circumstances can individuals accomplish more alone?
5. What are some characteristics besides interdependence that make groups successful?

Additional Sharing Circle Topics

A Group I Like Belonging To

We Cooperated to Get It Done

A Skill or Talent I Brought to the Team

A Time I Let the Team Down

A Role I Play in Groups

My Favorite Team

Something I Did That Helped the Team Succeed

A Way I Show Respect for Others

We Compromised to Get It Done

When the Easy Way Out Made Things Worse

Conflict Resolution

Activities in this unit teach students to:

- observe a series of real conflicts, drawing conclusions about their origins and methods used to resolve them.

- learn and practice eight conflict resolution strategies.

- recognize behaviors which tend to escalate and de-escalate conflicts.

Sharing Circles in this unit allow students to:

- examine and discuss real conflicts they have experienced.

- recognize how anger generated by a conflict incident can be transferred to and affect other relationships.

Conflict du Jour
Observations and Discussion

Objectives:
The students will:
—describe five conflicts that they have observed.
—identify and evaluate the conflict resolution strategies and methods used.

Materials:
one copy of the "Conflict Observation Sheet" for each student; chalkboard and chalk

Procedure:
Distribute the "Conflict Observation Forms." Go over the instructions.

Explain that the students are to observe five conflicts, one each day for a school week. The observed conflicts may occur between students at school, family members at home, characters on a TV show, etc.

Stress that the students are not to get involved; they are to observe silently. After each conflict, the students should immediately record observations and answer the questions on the form.

Note: Tell the students that they are *not* to identify people by name in their written observations.

The following week, ask the students to take out their completed observation forms. Have them form groups of four to six and share their observations. Ask the groups to tally the number of times each method or strategy was used to end a conflict. Have the groups report their findings while you record numbers and observations on the board. Facilitate discussion.

Discussion Questions:
1. How did you feel when you were observing other people's conflicts?
2. What kinds of things did people most often do that were helpful?
3. What kinds of things did people do that were hurtful?
4. What kinds of things were least effective?
5. How will your own methods of handling conflict change as a result of completing this activity?

Extension:
Have the students role play some of the conflicts, first using the resolution/ending they observed, and then using a more effective strategy.

Conflict Observations
Experience Sheet

Directions: Observe one conflict every day for five days. As soon as you can after the conflict has ended, answer the following questions. *Do not use names.*

Monday

What was the conflict about?

_____

How many people were involved?_____

Describe what happened: _____

_____

_____

Check all methods that were used to resolve or end the conflict:

___ fight or argument   ___ putting it off   ___ apologizing
___ sharing or taking turns   ___ humor   ___ compromise
___ asking for help   ___ problem solving or   ___ other
                                   negotiation

Tuesday

What was the conflict about?

_____

How many people were involved?_____

Describe what happened: _____

_____

_____

Check all methods that were used to resolve or end the conflict:

___ fight or argument   ___ putting it off   ___ apologizing
___ sharing or taking turns   ___ humor   ___ compromise
___ asking for help   ___ problem solving or   ___ other
                                   negotiation

Wednesday

What was the conflict about?

_____

How many people were involved?_____

Describe what happened: _____

_____

Check all methods that were used to resolve or end the conflict:

___ fight or argument   ___ putting it off   ___ apologizing
___ sharing or taking turns   ___ humor   ___ compromise
___ asking for help   ___ problem solving or   ___ other
                                   negotiation

Thursday

What was the conflict about?

_____

How many people were involved?_____

Describe what happened: _____

_____

Check all methods that were used to resolve or end the conflict:

___ fight or argument   ___ putting it off   ___ apologizing
___ sharing or taking turns   ___ humor   ___ compromise
___ asking for help   ___ problem solving or   ___ other
                                   negotiation

Friday

What was the conflict about?

_____

How many people were involved?_____

Describe what happened: _____

_____

Check all methods that were used to resolve or end the conflict:

___ fight or argument   ___ putting it off   ___ apologizing
___ sharing or taking turns   ___ humor   ___ compromise
___ asking for help   ___ problem solving or   ___ other
                                   negotiation

Exploring Alternatives to Conflict
Dramatizations and Discussion

Objectives:

The student will:

—learn and practice specific strategies for resolving conflict.

—demonstrate the use of conflict strategies in dramatizations.

Materials:

a copy of one scenario (from the list below) for each group of students; one copy of the experience sheet, "Conflict Resolution Strategies," for each student

Procedure:

On the board, write the heading "Strategies for Resolving Conflict." Explain to the students that in conflict situations, certain kinds of behaviors tend to help people solve their problems. List the strategies shown below, and make sure that the students understand them. Give examples, and ask the students to describe problems that might be resolved by using each alternative.

- Sharing: Using/doing something with another person.
- Taking turns: Alternately using/doing something with another person.
- Active listening: Hearing the other person's feelings or opinions.
- Postponing: Deciding to put off dealing with the conflict until another time.
- Using humor: Looking at the situation in a comical way; making light of the situation.
- Compromising: Giving up part, in order to get the remainder, of what you want.
- Expressing regret: Saying that you are sorry about the situation, without taking the blame.
- Problem solving: Discussing the problem; trying to find a mutually acceptable solution.

Divide the class into small groups and give each group a written conflict scenario. Instruct the groups to discuss the scenario and pick a conflict management strategy from the list of alternatives on the board. Have the members of each group act out the conflict and its resolution, while the rest of the class tries to guess which alternative they are using.

Conflict Scenarios

- Your group is working on a social studies project. You are drawing and coloring a map of the original 13 colonies. As a final step, you plan to print the names and founding dates of the colonies, along with the title of the map. However, another group member also wants to do the printing. The two of you start arguing about who should get the job and other group members take sides. The situation becomes very tense and noisy and the project is in danger of being ruined. Your teacher approaches the group and warns you to solve the problem — or forget the project.

• You plan to go to the movies on Saturday afternoon with a friend. Your family suddenly decides to hold a yard clean-up on Saturday, and this makes you very upset. You start to argue with your parents, insisting that since you have done your chores all week, you deserve to spend your allowance on a Saturday afternoon movie. Besides, your friend's parent has offered to drive you to and from the movie theater. You are in danger of being put on restriction because you are starting to yell at your parents.

• Without realizing it, you dropped (and lost) your homework on the way to school. That has put you in a bad mood. At recess, a classmate accidentally hits you in the back with a soccer ball. You react in anger and threaten to beat up your classmate after school. This makes the classmate angry and s/he reluctantly agrees to fight. Other classmates cheer. They are ready to stay after school to watch the fight. During lunch, you have a chance to think about it. Your realize that you picked the fight because you were upset about your lost homework. You didn't like being hit by the ball, but think that maybe it isn't worth a fight.

• You make plans with a few friends to meet a half hour before school to play a quick game of soccer in the school yard. You get up early, but decide to play Nintendo instead of meeting your friends. When you get to school, your friends are angry. They say you messed up the game by making one of the teams a person short. They start to accuse you of letting them down, but before they can express their feelings, you start making excuses. You don't give them a chance to talk. They start to walk away.

• Two students share a locker at school. One of the students is in a rush one day and unknowingly leaves the locker open. When the second student discovers the open locker an hour later, a jacket, a pair of sneakers, and a cassette tape are missing. The second student blames the first, who denies responsibility. They start to fight.

At the conclusion of the role plays, lead a class discussion.

Discussion Questions:

1. Why is it better to practice positive alternatives, rather than wait for a conflict to occur and then try them?
2. Which strategies are hardest to use and why? Which are easiest? Which work best and why?
3. At what point do you think you should get help to resolve a conflict?

Conflict Resolution Strategies
Experience Sheet

Have you ever been in a conflict? Of course! No matter how much you try to avoid them, conflicts happen. They are part of life. What makes conflicts upsetting and scary is not knowing how to handle them. If you don't know something helpful to do, you may end up making things worse. So study these strategies, and the next time you see a conflict coming, try one!

1. Share.
Whatever the conflict is over, keep (or use) some of it yourself, and let the other person have or use some.

2. Take turns.
Use or do something for a little while. Then let the other person take a turn.

3. Active Listen.
Let the other person talk while you listen carefully. Really try to understand the person's feelings and ideas.

4. Postpone.
If you or the other person are very angry or tired, put off dealing with the conflict until another time.

5. Use humor.
Look at the situation in a comical way, without poking fun at the other person. If you make light of the situation, be sure that the joke's on you.

6. Compromise.
Offer to give up part of what you want; ask the other person to do the same.

7. Express regret.
Say that you are sorry about the situation, without taking the blame.

8. Problem solve.
Discuss the problem and try to find a solution that is acceptable to both you and the other person.

Up and Down Escalators
Raising and Lowering the Level of Conflict

Objectives:
The students will:
—identify behaviors that escalate and de-escalate conflict.
—practice using communication skills to control the escalation of conflicts.

Materials:
paper and black marking pens

Procedure:
In your own words, introduce the concept of conflict *escalation* and *de-escalation*. For example, say:

Imagine an escalator, such as the kind you use in department stores. An escalator moves people up and down from one level to another. The same is true with behaviors that escalate and de-escalate conflict. Some words and actions raise, or escalate, the conflict to higher levels; other behaviors lower, or de-escalate the conflict, to lower levels. In judging the effects of certain behaviors on conflict, try to picture whether the behavior is making the conflict go up or down.

Distribute paper and marking pens. Ask the students to draw a large, bold arrow on the paper. When they have finished, tell them that you are going to read them two scenarios. As you read, they are to listen closely to the statements and actions of each character in the scenario. When they hear a statement or action that is likely to escalate the conflict, they should hold their arrow high, pointing up. When they hear a statement or action that is likely to de-escalate the conflict, they should hold their arrow pointing down.

Read each scenario slowly, allowing time for the students to respond. Notice if any of the behaviors draw mixed reactions from the students. After you have read each scenario, go back and role play the parts that caused disagreement, with volunteers taking the two roles. Demonstrate and discuss how voice tone, facial expression, and body posture contribute greatly to determining whether a specific behavior is escalating or de-escalating.

Conclude the activity with a general discussion of the concept of conflict escalation and de-escalation.

Extension:
After you have completed the readings and role plays, ask the students to suggest a typical conflict situation that they might face. Write a brief statement describing the situation on the board. Then ask volunteers to role play the characters in the scenario. As director, start the action by feeding the actors some initial dialogue. Then get the class involved, asking volunteers to call out lines that either escalate or de-escalate the conflict. Coach and experiment to demonstrate the effects of various types of actions and statements.

Scenarios:

• Ken and Sue are supposed to be working together to solve a math problem. Ken takes the problem sheet and starts to write his solution on it.

Sue: "Here, let me have that. I think I know how to do this." (Slides the paper away from Ken and starts to write on it.)

Ken: "Hey, I was right in the middle of something. Give that back to me." (Reaches over, pulls the paper back and continues writing.)

Sue: "You're not doing it right, dummy. You're going to have to erase the whole thing."

Ken: "I'll erase your face in a minute if you don't stop bugging me."

Sue: "We're supposed to be doing this together, and you're not listening to me!"

Ken: "Maybe I'd listen if you weren't so pushy. Anyway, I've finished it. There!"

Sue: "It's wrong. You can't prove your answer."

Ken: "Sure I can."

Sue: "Show me, Mr. Smartie. You couldn't prove it if you worked all day. Ha ha ha (loudly)."

Ken: "Shut up, Sue. You always think you know everything, but you don't" (Pushes Sue away.)

• Sergio and Livier are brother and sister. Sergio is watching TV. Livier walks in, picks up the remote control and changes the channel.

Sergio: "Why did you change the channel? I was watching that show!"

Livier: "I don't have time to argue with you. I have to watch this show for my science homework."

Sergio: "I don't care what it's for. That was my favorite show. Change it back right now!"

Livier: "You can't make me. I have just as much right to this TV as you do."

Sergio: "Not if I'm here first. I'm telling Mom!"

Livier: "Go ahead and tell Mom, cry baby. She'll just make you go do your homework."

Sergio: "I finished mine. What's the science program about?"

Livier: "Insects. Like you, creepy brother."

Discussion Questions

1. What types of behaviors almost always escalate a conflict?
2. What types of behaviors have a good chance of de-escalating a conflict?
3. Do you think being aware of whether a conflict is escalating or de-escalating can help you control the conflict? How?
4. What have you learned from this activity that will make a difference in the way you handle conflict?

I Got Into a Conflict
A Sharing Circle

Objectives:

The students will:

—describe conflicts they have experienced and what caused them.

—describe ways of dealing with the feelings of others in conflict situations.

—identify strategies for resolving conflicts with peers and adults.

Introduce the Topic:

Our topic today is, "I Got Into a Conflict." Conflicts are very common. They occur because of big and little things that happen in our lives. And sometimes the littlest things that happen can lead to the biggest conflicts. This is your opportunity to talk about a time when you had an argument or fight with someone. Maybe you and a friend argued over something that one of you said that the other didn't like. Or maybe you argued with a brother or sister over what TV show to watch, or who should do a particular chore around the house. Have you ever had a fight because someone broke a promise or couldn't keep as secret? If you feel comfortable telling us what happened, we'd like to hear it. Describe what the other person did and said, and what you did and said. Tell us how you felt and how the other person seemed to feel. There's just one thing you shouldn't tell us and that's the name of the other person, okay? Take a few moments to think about it. The topic is, "I Got Into a Conflict."

Discussion Questions:

1. How did most of us feel when we were part of a conflict?
2. What kinds of things led to the conflicts that we shared?
3. How could some of our conflicts have been prevented?
4. What conflict management strategies could have been used in the situations that we shared?

I Was Angry at One Person, But Took It Out on Someone Else
A Sharing Circle

Objectives:

The students will:

—describe conflicts that were started by misplaced anger.

—recognize that the initial conflict may still exist even after the secondary conflict is resolved.

Introduce the Topic:

Our topic today is, "I Was Angry at One Person, But Took It Out on Someone Else." This sort of thing happens quite a lot. Try to recall a time when you felt very angry at someone but, rather than express your anger to that person, you carried the bad feelings with you and then blew up at someone who didn't deserve it. Perhaps you were angry at a parent, a teacher, or some other adult, and were afraid to express your feelings. Our maybe your were angry at a classmate or a brother or sister. Without mentioning any names, tell us what caused you to be angry, and describe how the innocent person triggered your pent-up feelings. Think about it for a few moments. The topic is, "I Was Angry at One Person, But Took It Out on Someone Else."

Discussion Questions:

1. Why didn't you express your anger at the person who caused it?
2. What was the reaction of the innocent person on whom you dumped your anger?
3. When did you realize that you took out your feelings on the wrong person?
4. What are some strategies for resolving conflicts started by dumping on innocent people?

Additional Sharing Circle Topics

I Got Blamed for Something I Didn't Do
How Conflict Makes Me Feel
A Time When Sharing Prevented a Fight
How I Helped a Friend Resolve a Conflict
I Got Into a Fight Because I Was Already Feeling Upset
A Time I Was Afraid to Face a Conflict
Something That Really Bothers Me
I Observed a Conflict
A Time When I Was Involved in a Misunderstanding
A Time Someone Put Me Down But I Handled It Well
I Accidentally Made Somebody Mad
I Started a Conflict Between My Friends
A Time Humor Saved the Day
We Resolved a Conflict By Ourselves
A Time I Listened Well to Someone I Disagreed With